EMPATHY AT WORK

EMPATHY AT WORK

MIMI NICKLIN

EMBASSY BOOKS
www.embassybooks.in

First Edition 2024
Published in India by:
Embassy Book Distributors
120, Great Western Building, Maharashtra Chamber of
Commerce Lane, Fort, Mumbai 400 023, India
Tel: (+9122) -30967415, 22819546
Email: info@embassybooks.in
www.embassybooks.in

ISBN: 978-81-19726-43-1

Printed & bound in India by Parksons Graphics Pvt. Ltd.

DEDICATION

This book was a gift to myself in a time when I needed to see the bigger picture. But the energy to keep writing was a gift from others. I dedicate it to some very special people. **To my dad**, because I have spent fifteen years trying to follow in his footsteps. He is my hero. **To my mum** because so many of her words throughout my life are found in these pages and in my soul. **To my sister, Sophie**, because without her I would only ever be half. **And to my friend**, Tess, who will never know how much she impacted my life in the months when these words hit the page. Finally, **to my teams**, to the people who for many years have made my work worthwhile. To those I pitched with, and laughed with, stayed up all night with, and rewrote cost proposals with. So many of you shared words and actions that encouraged me to keep going.

You are always with me wherever I fly and you have inspired me to always work for those under my care and not the other way around.

FOREWORD

We often do this one exercise in our problem solving workshops, whether they be in rural communities or with multimillionaires and policymakers in big cities. We prompt every participant to remove their right shoe and ask the person next to them to put it on.

Shock and horror leads to shrieks of laughter as feet too big for high heels and too small for Oxfords bring out the child in all of us. And then the penny drops. Empathy is a very human, very shared experience.

While it can be uncomfortable and unfamiliar to wear someone else's shoes, empathy is a human capability we each have. But like all capabilities, it needs to be developed to be useful. Empathy is a capability our world needs to nurture now more than ever because, as this book will explain in detail shortly, we are facing an extreme empathy deficit.

Mimi Nicklin and I share a deep commitment to harnessing the power of empathy to make our worlds much better places. Mimi does a great job of slipping us into the shoes of a young British single mum taking on a business turnaround assignment in a region far from her own. She shares just enough of the emerging neuroscience to explain why and how empathy works as a leadership tool. But what connects with me is her ability to bring us into the trenches with her as she puts empathy into action, successfully rebuilding an enterprise with purpose and profit.

A friend who places C-suite executives in top companies worldwide says that nine out of every ten search briefs he gets require candidates show a demonstrated ability to build an empathetic organisation. Mimi's lessons are useful to anyone aspiring to those top spots.

Like Mimi, I come from the marketing world. I left a 20-year creative career on five continents to create a start-up in Sub-Saharan Africa. My company, Matchboxology, is designed to help wrestle with the life and death healthcare and community development problems facing the world's most vulnerable populations. The magic ingredient in our work is an ability to quickly develop a deep empathy with those closest to these problems. This is exactly what Mimi did with her colleagues and clients, too. So, what brought Mimi and I together was a serendipitous discovery that we both have built our careers on an ability to use empathy to stimulate behaviour changes.

Whether you are working on big thorny challenges that might save lives, or building purpose-led organisations that generate secure profit for sustainability, this book will teach you lessons you can apply immediately. Mimi and I passionately share a goal; we want to reverse the empathy deficit because we have seen with our own eyes what that can do for the world. We are confident that if you read this book, we're one person closer to our goal!

Cal Bruns is the co-founder of Matchboxology, Africa's first Human Centered Design consultancy and a regular contributor to empathy for impact discussions worldwide.

May this book be the beginning of your own conversation and practice of humanity's greatest leadership trait. May it be a reminder that in practising empathy you will always be doing the right thing. For your business, for your team, and for the world.

WHAT'S AHEAD...

"WOULDN'T IT BE WONDERFUL IF WE COULD ALL BE A LITTLE MORE GENTLE WITH EACH OTHER, AND A LITTLE MORE LOVING, HAVE A LITTLE MORE EMPATHY, AND MAYBE WE'D LIKE EACH OTHER A LITTLE BIT MORE."

JUDY GARLAND, ACTRESS, AS QUOTED IN
LITTLE GIRL LOST *(1974)*

PROLOGUE

Empathy in India & South Asia is Rising.

In awareness, practice, and commitment.
Across industries, categories, communities.
In boardrooms, courtrooms and every other space that humans gather.
This is good news. For this is a survival skill we cannot live without.
But is it rising quickly enough to solve our $8.8 Trillion problem at work?
This question is where this book begins.

I stood at the side of the stage and looked out at the 1000 faces surrounding the circular set up, feeling more nervous than was usual for me. The lights were a neon blue and there was smoke coming from the sides of the stage. There were so many screens I couldn't count them, and between them was a ballroom of Indian business leaders doing a post lunch revitalisation exercise that consisted of learning Punjabi dancing from a large animated man on the stage. Contrary to the seriousness that the sea of black and grey suits would portray, the audience was alive with energy, and for a moment the 'corporate' world they were all gathered in, faded into a tide of shared humanity. For a brief moment, as the beat of Bhangra united them, we were all connected.

I was in Bangalore and this was the first time that I had been flown across the world on an all-expenses paid trip, to speak on stage about organisational empathy and transformational leadership. My future was playing out, and it was India that was creating the rhythm.

As a professional, India has always been in my soul. An undeniable connection to all that makes this vast nation what it is. Working within the loud boardrooms, that home the endless vibrancy of debate that can only be found within its borders, has led many of my career choices to date. As I write we are in the process of launching India's first organisational empathy platform and I am committed to making a lasting contribution to the people and future of the tiger of the continent.

On that day in Bangalore, I was about to present to one of the oldest established and largest Fortune 500 businesses in the world, Aditya Birla. I was 100% present in that reality and in the sheer size of the achievement, and whilst my nerves were present so was my passion. As the lights flashed, the crowd clapped and the upbeat tone of the TV-famous MC ran through my bio, the scale was not lost on me. The 360-degree stage called and the an older man in a turban smiled back at me as I caught his eye. I was exactly where I was meant to be, of that I was sure, but was India ready for me? Ready for empathy? What if they didn't like it? What if one of those tens of screens, failed? What if, what if, what if?

As I waited for the MC to get to the part where she announced "*please welcome Mimi Nicklin to the stage*" I was stuck somewhere between immense pride and a deep apprehension about tripping up the steps to a stage reminiscent of large music event - steep, sparkling with lights and elevated above eye level. My name called, my heels stepped up the stairs, and the screens around me beamed back with my picture in real time up front and centre. The corporate 'Empathy Everywhere' journey was now in full swing, in a country that was three months away from meeting its predicted moment of becoming the world's most populous nation. If a difference to our shared humanity, in terms of reconnecting our workplaces and world, starts anywhere, it needed to be here.

THE ROOTS OF THE ROAD

The truth is that I never thought about becoming an author or a 'thought leader' until I wrote my first book 'Softening the Edge'. When it became a bestseller, days before it hit the shelves of any store, I sat in total shock looking at the position of my book up there ahead of Malcolm Gladwell with a deep sense that I was creating something which would change my life and hopefully, the lives of many others. My words were in the world, people were reading them, and it was too late to take them back now. My leadership soul and philosophy were out there for all to critique within a business turnaround story that not everyone would appreciate me publishing. Writing books based on true stories is not for the faint hearted and the two years behind me hadn't been easy. Place on top of that the fact that 'empathy' was still deeply misunderstood (and often still is) and unaccepted in the Asian working world, and I knew that the road ahead was clearly going to be a lonely one. At least for a while.

I started to write about empathy, its influence, and the decreasing levels of it we see in the world of work and society in 2019. I was struck by the terrible levels of loneliness, the suicide rates, the burnout, the corporate anxiety, the apathy, and the absenteeism. The lack of productivity. All compressed by the fact that we didn't seem to be looking for a solution for these silent monsters as they swept our office corridors. The world of work hadn't yet recognised what was ahead. But then, how could they? No one knew what 2020-2023 would bring and we were all entirely unprepared and still blissfully unaware.

EMPATHY AT SPEED

Five years later and having now studied, created and consulted in this field, amongst some of Asia and the world's largest brands, this new edition of that original book, recreated, updated and republished for India and South Asia, is a natural next step for me. I deeply believe that "*The More That The World Talks About Empathy, The More Empathy The World Will Have*", so writing one book was never going to be an option, plus a 'one size fits all' approach goes against the principles of empathy themselves - especially when it comes to content that will resonate in the Indian corporate world.

In 2016 the Harvard Business Review released it's Empathy Index, under which it has published two different lists of companies - the top 20, and the least 20, most empathetic companies. At the time, Indian companies strongly made their presence felt in the list of the least empathetic list. Today this is changing and some of the world's most connected organisations and leaders are coming out of India with Satya Nadella of Microsoft and Indira Nooyi, ex-Pepsi Co, leading the way and putting modern Indian leadership into the spotlight.

It was President Obama who told us that '*we should be thinking about our empathy deficit*" back in 2006 and since then political and organisational leaders, the world over, are adapting their leadership style and listening to their people. Today it's not a matter of "when" but "how" do we adapt more organisations to the recognition that their people must come first. This is humanism and capitalism in balance and there are an abundance of businesses yet to achieve this consistently.

Throughout my entire career I have been passionate about the sustainable wellness of our workforce and the future of inclusive leadership that promotes human values, beyond the financial value, of every business. This work addresses the Global Empathy Deficit from within our organisations and approaches the solve to our $8.8 Trillion[1] loss in productivity annually due to disengagement in our teams. Gallup has surveyed 2.2 million employees since 2009 - approximately 160,000 per year - and their data shows today that only 23% of the workforce is engaged. That leaves over 75% of your staff underperforming, disconnected and considering resignation (the data also shows that 51% of them[2] are considering resigning.) A loss of $8,8 trillion suddenly seems far more realistic that we might have thought.

Are we doing enough to actively turn this all around?

As Jacinda Arden resigned from her position of Prime Minister of New Zealand in early 2023 the conversation about empathetic leadership, as a force for progress and success in ever evolving tough circumstances, reached fever pitch. The business media has since exploded with content aiding leadership and HR teams in information and training to elevate the way they communicate with, and understand, their teams. The requirement for Indian leaders who listen and understand their audiences has been finally recognised as the need of the hour, but also the need for the future. We have reached a point as a business community where the Empathy Deficit is changing our ability to connect with each other at dangerously low levels. Our collective loneliness, segregation

[1] https://www.gallup.com/workplace/393497/world-trillion-workplace-problem.aspx

[2] https://www.gallup.com/workplace/506819/half-employees-looking-leave.aspx

and disconnection is impacting our lifespan as well as our career success. Our loneliness is killing us[3] and professional attrition is draining our profits in the home market and abroad.[4]

"I'm proudly focused on empathy because leaders can be both empathetic and strong. What the world needs now is clearly the quality of empathy." Jacinda Ardern, Davos.

From politicians to doctors, CEOs to activists, many are still significantly underestimating the powerfully impressive role increased belonging and empathy could be be having on our organisational return and the lack of progress is threatening our speed of growth.

I define leadership in this book widely. After all, leaders can and should, be found in all walks of life, in large organisations, small start-ups, schools, political parties, across communities, and within religious institutions. Wherever you lead in India, more empathy, connection and a commitment to listening, and to walking in the shoes of those around you, will go a very long way to building and rebuilding long-lasting and effective relationships. Today, too many people still miscalculate the power that empathy has to impact their organisations and their bottom line.

My curiosity around how empathy can solve leadership and social challenges across the country - and bring out better performance and relationships - has naturally led to more and more people asking me how to apply this in the areas that impact our organisational success the most. I now travel to India up to ten times a year working with leaders to drive the transformational emotional intelligence and listening skills that their multi-generational and culturally-diverse employees demand. From Aditya Birla and Big Basket, to Stellantis and Hindustan Unilever, the passion and belief in these leadership shifts is

[3] https://www.usatoday.com/story/news/health/2023/12/24/loneliness-epidemic-u-s-surgeon-general-solution/71971896007/

[4] https://www.mckinsey.com/capabilities/people-and-organizational-performance/our-insights/the-great-attrition-is-making-hiring-harder-are-you-searching-the-right-talent-pools

both as heartening as it is required. There are few countries on earth as diverse - in language, culture, customs, habits, political opinion, regions and even consumption - as India, and therefore this need for unity and understanding in leadership here, is ever higher.

India's vision of becoming a "developed nation" by 2047[5] and all the efficiency realities that come with that, relies on sound public policymaking and leadership that understands their changing nation. These policies will be the building blocks that shape society, promote progress, and, ultimately, lead as many of the 1.2 billion people as possible, forward, together. However, for these policies to succeed, we need leaders who understand the people they serve and practice empathetic leadership in their delivery and action.

I hope this book encourages all who read it to more consistently practice this exact skillset. A skillset for the business world that can help us lead, engage and perform better by using an ability that we have evolved to use, with our fellow humans, over hundreds of thousands of years and yet have allowed to slowly disappear before our very eyes.

[5] Viksit Bharat @ 2047

Chapter 1

THE LOVE OF THE HOURS THAT MAKE US OUR MONEY

"I love my job."

Wouldn't it be wonderful if more people could say that and truly mean it? Given that we spend over a third of our lives at work, this should be less of a 'nice to have' and more of a 'must have', yet time and time again we consider job fulfilment a luxury rather than an essential.

Why is it that in a world of so many forward-thinking leaders and innovators, we don't feel compelled to enforce in our working environments the same social responsibilities and behaviours that we value in our personal lives? Why can people behave badly, without respect, under the guise of 'business'? And how did we let 'corporate culture' overrule the norms of our own personal standards?

Did you know that in a Deloitte study in 2016 it was concluded that 87 percent of people have "no passion for their work" at all?[i] This is a soul-crushing percentage of the population getting up and going to work without any heart to do so. Not only does this make for an entirely unfulfilled working population, but in response, the number of people leaving organisations to set up their own entrepreneurial endeavours, or simply to pursue their 'side hustle' full time, is going forever up.[ii]

Leaving the corporate world has become the way for many people to try and improve the love of the hours that make us our money. However, is it all it's made out to be? And what are we doing to stop our top talent setting up alone? These are questions that concern me, and I cannot understand how we are letting it happen with so few people freaking out about it! If people continue to flow out of the corporate world for smaller businesses, what does that mean for the long-term quality of thought and innovation within the companies that have the resources to make an immediate global impact? And how will these bigger, legacy-led, companies remain competitive?

I have seen many people—I have been one of them—leave the corporate world for smaller, entrepreneurial work, and although they may gain in many areas, people aren't fully aware of the price they pay for going it alone. We are losing people to this 'grass is greener' freelance life, but quite frankly we don't know the wider impact on them or the industries they leave behind. The age of exit is getting younger as Millennials and Gen Z's simply won't stand for suboptimal working environments—and who can blame them?—but the other side of this is that their professional development dwindles from the moment they leave. They no longer have a boss to guide them, a senior leader to massage an idea to perfection, or anyone with experience to gift them with wise words or memory of a situation to intuitively solve an issue. By all accounts, the level of personal growth slows down and connectivity to a wider 'village' crashes as non-office-based work-life takes root. The move may turn out to be a blazing success, but meanwhile these newly 'freed' entrepreneurs and freelancers are even more alone than they were before, and the organisations they leave behind are poorer by another talented mind.

Empathy is the commitment to using your imagination to join another person's world with the sole and deep desire to understand them.

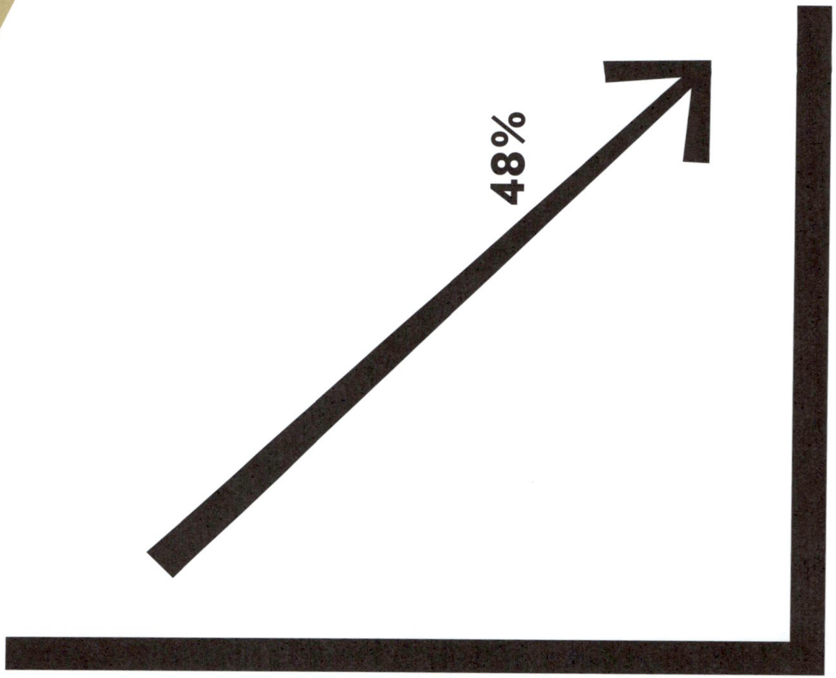
48%

THE EMPATHY DEFICIT

BETWEEN 1979 AND 2009

I recently asked one of our interns what the majority of his friends were doing and what their goals were. He replied that only two of them were going into corporate internships because the feeling today is that they can "do it better alone". They don't believe that senior players in organisations are able to, or interested in, trying to understand them, so why bother with corporate life? If the middle is leaving for freelance life, though, and the bottom is opting out before they begin, it won't take the top long to realise that the gap in empathetic understanding of their teams is systematically choking their talent pipeline. Reducing the stress culture and empathising with our people is not an option; it's an imperative to sustaining organisational unity. A resolution is possible, and cultivating motivation to work toward that resolution should be the number one point on the agenda for all leaders in all walks of social, political, and corporate life. **The ripples of corporate change can only start with us.**

THE EMPATHY DEFICIT

After thirty years of data collection that shows empathy is declining, we have a deficit on our hands, a corporate humanity deficit, an **Empathy Deficit.**[iii] The Empathy Deficit has been formed by a gap in connection with each other at the deepest social levels over many decades, and it undermines the fundamental principles of humanity's ability to thrive. Between 1979 and 2009 we saw empathy decline by 48 percent, with a particularly steep decline between 2000 and 2009.[iv] As our modern urban and technologically driven lives continue to separate us from our natural connected state as human beings, this decline is perilous for society. The Empathy Deficit we see creates a gap in understanding and a gap between us all, creating far more 'us and them' relationships than 'me and you' relationships. Sitting back and watching this trend continue should not be an option. Are we really resigned to the fact that this downward spiral to an ever more disparate, transactional, and egocentric environment is simply a sign of modern day living and our future? I for one am not.

The good news? Due to the neuro plasticity of our brains, empathy is a skill we can learn, fine tune, and practise. Contrary to the belief of many, it is not a trait we may or may not be born with but a skill we can hone and improve. Changing our society and our organisations to become more connected, open, and thriving is entirely within our grasp. Sitting back and watching this Empathy Deficit grow, creating gaps that extend to all social engagements and organisational constructs—between bosses and their teams, between teammates and their colleagues, and between the C-Suite and those who run their businesses daily—should not be a negative movement we allow to continue. We are witnessing an Empathy Deficit that is causing a growing emotional intelligence gap at all levels of life. Not only is this a tragedy for us as people, it could become a threat to our species!

TODAY'S LOW EMPATHY REALITY

The fourth revolution is upon us, and we now seem to spend more time on a screen than we do sleeping. Virtual connections, high-stress environments, shared workspaces, and an always-connected cell phone mean that employees are closer together than ever before, and yet we are suffering with the highest levels of loneliness in history. Workplace absenteeism and apathy are reaching endemic proportions. Anxiety, depression, and epidemic levels of burnout complete the picture. According to the World Health Organisation, more than 322 million people have depression, and suicide rates are the highest they have been for half a century.[v]

This stark picture is where this book begins. So, why does it look this way?

Times have changed immeasurably since the decades of organisational systems and structures that put us on the behavioural track we follow today. If we take the time to step out of the daily grind to look at the impact of working life on people, on our CEOs and on our society at large, we leaders may realise we are set to lose the best of our people, and the best of our work, without knowing the wider long-term impact. The grass is most definitely not always greener outside of corporate life, but if we don't craft our own corporate fields into something that resembles a more modern definition of conscientious caretaking for our teams, we will find our best people running for assumed brighter pastures. **Never has there been a time in history when we needed an intervention into our working lives more than we do today.** As the environments we work within become ever tougher and sharper edged, and humanity seems to be conspiring into ever tighter micro groups fighting against different tides, we need to stop and take stock of where we are if we are to ensure we end up where we really want to be.

As I write, the world is arguably more of a burden on our lives, our souls, and our team discussions than it ever has been. There are insurmountable problems everywhere one looks, and as individuals we lie awake at night or stare blindly at the news, wondering how ever we might help solve them. Attacks in the Ukraine are ongoing, hurting the innocent as our screens fill with children suffering the most. The Indian government continues to apply perceived anti-Muslim laws and rhetoric to millions of people, South Africa watches xenophobic attacks that they thought they had ended years ago, prisoners in China sneak "*please help us*" messages into boxes of Christmas cards headed for the West, asking for the support of human rights lawyers. Over 5.6 million Syrian refugees have fled their borders to escape war, with 70 percent of them living far below the poverty line in camps or urban areas. Meanwhile, we see brutal war in Palestine and parts Africa continue as if they are unstoppable. As we reassess our working approach, we question daily whether the world of work will ever be quite the same again. And should it be?

This has become a time for en masse reassessment of our corporate lives and behaviour, our values and our goals. In recent history there has arguably not been a better, or more needed, time for us all to look at our social corporate cohesion with new eyes. It is time to firmly question the corporate reality we have become so accustomed to and ask if corporate life is truly fulfilling us and our teams as it should. Do we find joy in our work? **Are we happy?**

The world, and therefore the world of work, has been under siege (mainly from ourselves) for many years. We have a deep problem at the exact point where humanity meets capitalism, and there is a lack of balance between the two. This is a problem fuelled by three key parts.

First, an ubiquitous obsession with growth at all costs; second, a never-ending stress cycle that we have become accustomed to living and working within; and third, a widespread disconnection between the world's people at a scale never before witnessed. Many argue that the acute individualism, the unkindness, and the human attack has always been this way and that it is only now that the media is so omnipresent that we have full sight of humanity's actions. Whether this is accurate or not, the weight of our shared social behaviour is a heavy burden to bear.

The reality is that as the media increases the visibility of these behavioural and social issues we are much more aware of them, and that demands of us a responsibility to act upon that awareness. Every copy of the *Economist* or newspaper that you pick up, and every news site you scroll through, provides you with ever more evidence of these seismic shifts in human interaction and our subsequent detachment. This knowledge can be debilitatingly concerning and I, for one, have a deep desire to try and slow the momentum of these social shifts, or at least ease some of the corporate hurt.

The impact of the macro social behaviour on our micro corporate lives is ever present, and it feels like we are all far too comfortable with the status quo. At some point this needs to change. Perhaps that point is now?

After many months in 2020 that saw the world working from home, with time given back to us in the strangest of ways, we have had an opportunity for the first time in a long time to truly slow down. To pause and to consider our wider context. To review and reassess. This may have been time well spent in order to form a new, very much needed, perspective. We simply cannot continue to blindly *hope* that people's personal lives will not be inextricably impacted by the state that we have been working in. There are no boundaries between the two facets of our existence any longer. We live and we work, we work and we live, and this is a porous daily engagement where content and information from one naturally impacts the other. We can't expect our teams to not want to make change, to push back against old patterns and to want to work for a higher, more impactful purpose.

There is a lack of balance between humanity and capitalism. Why?

1. *An ubiquitous obsession with growth at all costs.*
2. *A never-ending stress cycle that we have become accustomed to living and working within.*
3. *A widespread disconnection between the world's people at a scale never before witnessed.*

Honestly, nor should we want them to. It is exactly this desire that will lead us to demand changes to both our corporate and individual lives, and health. These are the changes that we desperately need to see and that will lead our teams to constantly reassess why they are doing what they are doing, well beyond the rationale of a monthly pay cheque.

In our increasingly interconnected, transparent, and socially alive world, work and life are entirely complementary, they are in sync; individual changes lead to organisational change, and in turn organisational change has a direct impact on the larger world. Our commitment as leaders to changing our workplaces and organisations, one team of people at a time, is a direct commitment to taking steps to change something much bigger than just that one team or business alone. It is a committed leap toward making a difference to the hundreds of people connected to the organisation and the families, friends, supporting teams, and suppliers that your team impacts. Once upon a time we spoke of six degrees of separation between us, but today this is closer to two degrees. Impact internally directly creates impact externally, in an always-on, subconscious human dance.

With a firm commitment and an alignment between your business and humanity's goals, you can create a powerful *ripple* effect. **Being more empathetic will benefit the world: it's that simple.** Our ability as leaders to create ripples that reach beyond the walls we work within to affect people and society, often in an accumulation of small ways, is vastly underestimated. This ripple effect should be our driving force. As a Millennial myself, I know of the deep shared desire to create and practise a set of leadership and life principles that can actively soften the edges of the close circles of people around me. As the gap between the older generation of leaders and the more youthful, Millennial workforce widens, it will be leaders of my age and drive who can make significant change that impacts both the top of the organisational tree, as well as the bottom line of the businesses we steer. We are perfectly placed to lead the change. We are a generation that wakes up wanting to make a difference. We are committed to using our skills for greater good. We go to sleep dreaming of a change we can be part of, and although we know that we alone cannot change the world, we also know that our Millennial cohorts are entirely tracking with the fact that doing nothing is no longer an option.

Personally, I am starting in the only way I know how; to use my voice to try and enthuse more people to practise the empathetic leadership skills, and consciously regenerative behaviours, that can so powerfully change businesses and people's lives and health. I have seen these principles create impactful change across over twenty markets globally; environments I have been able to enter and witness flourish from empathetic engagements and leadership principles that deliberately put people above all else. The currencies I write of are empathy, emotional intelligence, and human understanding. Currencies that make up Regenerative Leadership and empathetic influence. Currencies that the world and our workplaces are desperately short on, even though the evidence in their support for growing business and profit is now widely known. Contrary to some beliefs, these are not 'soft' skills or talents, **these are the skills at the heart of the future of leadership**. Regenerative Leadership skills are focused on transforming and regenerating people and their organisational context by emotionally engaging with the key inputs they need to thrive as human beings. Leadership that is transformational in its ability to prepare businesses and teams for a new world of commerce and change, for home working, flexible formats, purpose-led goal setting, and cohesive sustainable agendas. These are tenets that recent times have proven to be more valid and more current than ever before. As we navigate a new decade, it is my prediction that **empathetic influence will be recognised as one of the most desired facets of inspirational and impactful leadership of our times.**

This book is about making a conscientious and empathetic change to your career or business. It looks at our commitment to creating more businesses that balance profit with positive change for the people that work within them. It defines how this new balance will ripple outward to make success something that is measured at the intersection of human *values* and business *value*. And finally, it uncovers the intersection of humanism and capitalism as a **new methodology for making money.**

I am writing for the leaders of businesses who want to be fit for purpose in today's Millennial-led world—a world of compassionate capitalism, consumption that **balances the kick of the ownership with the kindness of its creation**, and full of people looking for a sense of belonging, order, and direction in our turbulent and ever-changing global environment. I am writing for the leaders who are feeling unsure how to survive the new wave of Millennial and Gen Z demands that are rearranging the rules. I am writing for all people who want to practise a set of humanist skills with the belief that doing so is both valued and valuable, so that they can soften the edges of our corporate, social, and political environments to immense shared merit and growth.

All it takes to change the world is the conviction to do so. This book, and the stories I share within it, are my pursuit to bring conscientiousness and empathetic influence to the forefront of a few more discussions. I aim to find a way to bring more conviction to the practice of driving humanism into the capitalism of the world of work and industry as we know it. People *beyond* profit.

At times I err on the side of marketing and advertising, as these are the industries that I love, but the principles throughout *Empathy At Work* are as relevant to finance, law, politics or medicine; **they are simply principles of people**.

I am writing this book as a global citizen, a mother, a brand strategist, and a female creative leader. I am not an analyst, research specialist or an academic, but as a business leader and a lifelong purveyor of human emotions cross-culturally, I have the passion and the proof that the leverage of empathy in our workplaces **has commercial value** and an impressive impact on the workplace today.

Empathy is a data set and an input for your business and future of decision making. It is as valuable to your organisation today as the output you create. Without being able to walk in the shoes of others, to understand diverse viewpoints, it is nearly impossible to inspire and lead teams to success, and even harder to create marketing, powerful business decisions, or innovative products and services that truly and deeply resonate with people.

I don't want to create a "movement" or a fleeting moment, I want us to open up to a practice. A practice that we can commit to as our new normal.

Because in the end, **practice creates permanence.**

Chapter 2

WHAT IS EMPATHY AND DOES IT ALREADY EXIST IN THE CORPORATE WORLD?

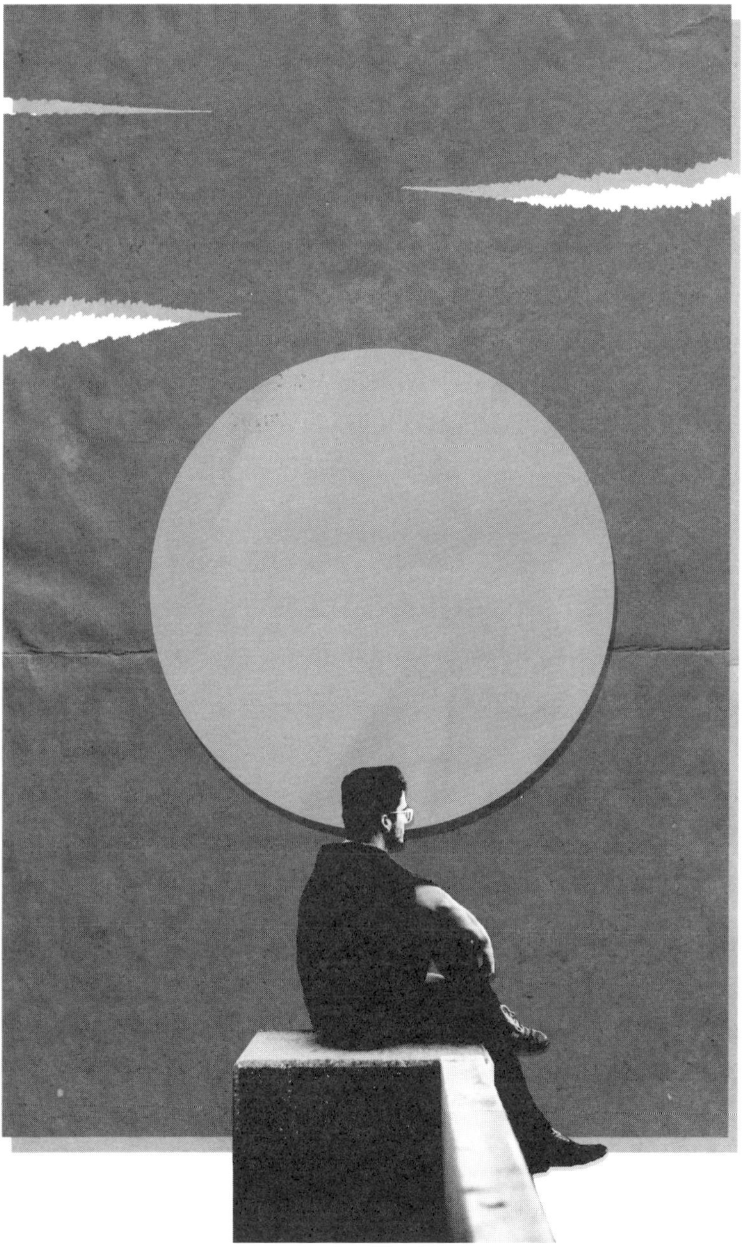

It was President Obama (prior to becoming president) who started talking about the Empathy Deficit publicly back in 2006 when he stated: *"There's a lot of talk in this country about the federal deficit, but I think we should talk more about our empathy deficit".*[viii] Today, we see the impact he was referring to, loud and clear.

I define leadership in this book extremely widely. After all, leaders can, and should, be found in all walks of life; in large organisations, small start-ups, schools, political parties, across communities, and within homes. Wherever you lead, more empathy and a commitment to listening, understanding, and to walking in the shoes of those around you will go a very long way to building and rebuilding sustainable, balanced, and fulfilling relationships. Today, far too many people underestimate the power that empathy has to impact their organisations and their bottom line. I hope this book encourages all who read it to more consistently practise the skills that we have evolved to use with our fellow humans over hundreds of thousands of years.

WHY EMPATHY AND WHY NOW?

In recent times, we so often push aside our natural empathetic response in the fury of a moment around a boardroom table or a debate over next best steps. If we could only talk about empathy a little more, the act of having those conversations holds the power to create much-needed change. It is empathy that has aided us in surviving and thriving as a population for nearly two hundred thousand years, and yet today we are seeing the deepest and most widespread deficit of this natural ability in all of human history. The question here is, can we recreate our working world to become a more connected and cohesive environment in which more of us truly love what we do? Can we stop the habitual momentum of putting profit above our people at all costs, before we fall over an edge too sharp to climb back over?

Before moving further into the impact of the global Empathy Deficit and what it means for us as people and as leaders, it is worth defining exactly what empathy is, because although it is a term we know, and that you may be using freely, it is so often confused with sympathy, compassion, or pity. Let's begin at the beginning.

DEFINING EMPATHY

Imagine watching your friend walk up to her car. She unlocks it remotely and slides in with her eyes on her phone. She is distracted. Somehow as she pulls the door shut she firmly slams her fingers in the car door, crushing her little finger and ripping the nail away from the skin. She screams out as blood begins to pour.

Did you flinch? Or close your fist around your little finger reactively? The odds are, you probably did. Every time I re-read my own paragraph my hands still curl in.

This is the simplest example of empathy in action. At its most basic, empathy is **the ability to recognise and respond to the reality, emotions, or pain of others.**[xv] It is the ability to put yourself into their place, to understand their context and to see things as they do. Flinching when you hear a story like this, physically feeling grief when you watch a terribly sad story on the news, or laughing with others are examples of our most natural, biologically imperative, empathetic response. For some this comes more naturally or quickly but we are all born with the ability to empathise. Have you ever cried in front of a small child or toddler? It is entirely natural for them to immediately respond by feeling sad themselves. Their faces soften, their mouths downturn, and their eyes fill with worry as they immediately ask, "*Do you feel sad?*" In the case of my daughter, who is two years old, she will then immediately move into action to try and make me laugh and smile and then hurry to ask, "*Are you happy again now, Mummy?*" In part, of course, this is due to her care for me as her mum, but beyond that you can also see her whole body lighten when I say "*yes*". The heaviness of her empathy for me when I appeared sad made her sad too. Although she really did want me to feel happy in myself, more-so she wanted her own sadness gone so she could get back to playing with her toys and laughing like a wild thing. Putting herself into my position is natural to her because empathy is natural to all of us. The reality is, however, we don't all choose to activate it all that often, especially at work.

THE ORIGINS OF EMPATHY

empathy | empəTH'ē

(n.) The ability to understand and share the feelings of another.

THE OXFORD ENGLISH DICTIONARY

The word *empathy* itself was originally inspired by both the Greek root pathos (meaning 'feeling', 'emotion', or 'suffering') and the German aesthetic term *Einfühlung*[ix] (meaning 'feeling into'). From the information I have found, Einfühlung was a word created specifically to express our unique ability to sense and to understand other people's emotions and context. As far as I can find, the term first appeared in the German philosopher Robert Vischer's 1873 dissertation where Vischer used the word to explore the human capacity to "personally enter" into a piece of art or literature and "feel" the emotions that the artist was trying to convey.[x] The work of any writer or creative mind is to create work that connects deeply enough with the viewer, reader, or audience that the original author can infuse the person's thoughts or influence their behaviour. My hope throughout this book is to do the same.

REGENERATING OUR PASSION FOR THE HOURS WE WORK

Did you know that we spend ninety thousand hours working during our lifetime?[xi] It begs the question as to why we are so willing to let our frustration or unhappiness during these hours slide. It is a monumental proportion of our lives and far too high a percentage to be dismissed so easily. How might *"I love my job"* really look for people if we were to reassess the reality we have been experiencing for so many years?

Picture this. You work in an office filled with people you actually want to spend time with because they were handpicked to work with each other. The team was not chosen based on a corporate outline in a handbook covering 'aligned values' that they 'should possess', but because each member had been hand selected to fit with the exact set of people they were being chosen to work with. The main hiring criteria is the happiness and fulfilment of those already there, and not the clients they will serve or the profit they will achieve. They are chosen for being 'the right people for our people' before all else.

You are trusted to work hard because your team knows you want to. Your work routines adapt to fit your lifestyle whilst ensuring that you offer the team the stability and support they need. Given you sincerely like them, you do this as second nature.

No one asks you why you are in late unless they are genuinely worried about your health or commute, and you don't have to ask to take off a Monday if you were at a client event all day Saturday. It is a given.

The office can be silent or noisy or anything in between; the team sets the energy and no one forces fun. No one shouts, no one chastises, and no one but you has authority over your work. This is a democracy but with decision making at its heart and action on the agenda.

Wins are shared, success is celebrated, and big failures are OK. Advice is given but at the end of the day, the management of your day is left to you. The idea that experience is the world's greatest teacher is concrete.

The CEO is entirely realistic about how the industry goes, accepting that you might work long hours, that your clients can be extremely tough, and that therefore being at work isn't always fun. They will also accept that, sometimes, work is not entirely where you want to be. This is understood and accepted in a culture that respects emotional agility and your need for space and time away from your desk.

There are break rooms for those times when you need to get away; a sign on the door reminds you that cortisol (the stress hormone) takes twenty minutes to reduce to normal levels and that you therefore need to take a proper pause to reap the benefits of the break.

The CEO and the leadership team sit within their team and they work the same hours that you do. They believe that the key to being a team is that you work *together* as a connected group marching to the same tune. No one works *for* anyone because you are all too busy working *with* each other.

You feel genuinely cared for. Your boss believes in you because they understand you, and you never doubt that. You know that you come first. When they listen, they hear you, and when they ask how you are, they mean it.

fig 1.

EMPATHY:
"I FEEL WHAT YOU FEEL. I FEEL YOUR PAIN."

fig 2.

SYMPATHY:

"I FEEL A SUPPORTIVE EMOTION ABOUT YOUR FEELINGS. I FEEL PITY FOR YOUR PAIN."

J. KEEN,
SCIENTIST AND ACADEMIC, 2006

"WHEREVER YOU LEAD, I BELIEVE THAT A TOUCH MORE EMPATHY, A COMMITMENT TO LISTENING, LEANING IN AND TO WALKING IN THE SHOES OF THOSE AROUND YOU, GOES A VERY LONG WAY TO BUILDING AND REBUILDING SUSTAINABLE, BALANCED AND FULFILLING RELATIONSHIPS."

MERRIAM WEBSTER DICTIONARY

empathy | empəTH'ē

(n.) The action of understanding, being aware of, being sensitive to, and vicariously experiencing the feelings, thoughts, and experience of another...

The most junior member of staff can sit opposite any leader if there happens to be a seat free. It doesn't cross anyone's mind that this could ever be an issue. People are people. Rank is invisible whereas experience and decision making are embraced.

Your family member is sick and you have to travel abroad; your first thought is "*how soon can I get there?*" and not "*will my boss let me go?*"

You are given your birthday off because who wants to spend their birthday in the office?

You watch your leadership team say *no* to the clients that come through the door and turn out not to be an ethical or cultural match, seeing the revenue walk out with them — regardless of the tension that exists around that month's cash flow.

As a team you fight for your fees, not because they are bulked up with additional hours, but because you can, in your heart, justify every penny being there for the clients' gain and their people's sanity and performance. You charge your worth and you know you are worth what you charge.

You believe in your boss when they say "*What can I do to help?*" because they always ask and they always help.

You are encouraged to learn and to innovate. The leadership team knows that, as humans, if we are growing, we are thriving.

Teams move around the office without asking permission and no one is going to ask them why, to inform HR or fill in a form. They are happy, and people accept that as it is.

You learn from your bosses. You genuinely want to be able to do what they do. They lead by example and practise what they preach.

This is not just team above all; this is a business built on people above all. This is a business that puts empathy at the heart of every daily decision aligned to human values *beyond* (not in place of) financial value. Behind each decision is empathy for people, for individuals and for the team. It is this empathetic understanding that is the powerful driving force in making a business one that people want to stay in.

These businesses exist, but they do not make up nearly enough of the workplaces worldwide today. Overall, the businesses that truly succeed are the ones that put their own **caring economy alongside the sharing economy** and make profit by doing so. They create a ripple every day.

These businesses are driven by knowing that "*I love my job*" is truly the ultimate revenue and success driver, within the corporate world and within life, and unsurprisingly these businesses grow faster than their counterparts. They recognise that the tougher the macroenvironment becomes, the faster we must improve our microenvironments to make up for it.

√16·x=8

Chapter 3

THE SCIENCE OF THE EMPATHY STORY

While pulling this book together, so much was the passion for the topic, I came across tens of people who asked me to finish writing before I even began. It feels like a 'now or never' moment that is gaining traction every hour., As I write, the instinctive and innate response from people across geographies and industries is for human connection and cohesion. The roots of empathy are in exactly this.

There are times, however, when I also find myself meeting a less enthusiastic group of people: naysayers. People who don't want to understand or hear of the opinions, media, or evidence surrounding empathetic influence and the impact of reconnecting to each other more authentically. People who don't believe humanity and emotional intelligence have any place in the world of Excel spreadsheets, boardroom tables, and revenue numbers. For these people, their work and the corporate world have never been that way and they are not open to changing things now. They have been conditioned in a more self-centred, self-fulfilling universe and have become accustomed to the power of one. Perhaps considering something new is too much work, or they have too little time, or it's simply uncomfortable, but in any case, they are not at all fans of this thinking (which is all the more reason to talk a little more loudly). I am not going to try and convince these people, but I will work to provide evidence of the power of empathy in driving business results and perhaps the results will speak for themselves. It will be the driving of awareness of Regenerative Leadership that puts empathy at the core of organisations and creates the opportunity to build business and human resilience to provoke impactful organisational results. Doing this at scale, over a period of time, will allow us to run our teams with empathy. This will eventually become a standard business practice engrained into leadership skillset development.

Throughout *Empathy At Work* I use the word 'practice' with clear intention. It is in the *practice* of becoming more empathetic that we connect with our natural ability to be more empathetic. For those with barriers up, it will be practice that allows the creation of the new evidence supporting their actions that shows them what this behavioural shift can instigate. The longstanding bestselling American author Joe Hyams beautifully summed up the impact of practice when he said: *"only through practice and more practice can you go on to do something without conscious effort."* [xii] The enduring goal for the corporate world should be to develop the **practice of empathy** with the knowledge that once we begin to practise at scale in the business world, the uptake from the humans around us will do the rest. From there, positive change will follow.

FROM BATTLEFIELDS TO BOARDROOMS

Often, empathy is mistaken as a 'soft' skill, or misinterpreted as a skillset saved for charity donation and child welfare campaigns, and some people see empathy as a facet saved only for overly emotional or nurturing environments such as the healthcare system. This couldn't be further from the truth and this chapter will provide compelling references and evidence for the leverage of empathy on an organisational scale. With that in mind, I am starting with the military because if the world's armies see the proof and power of empathy in achievement and optimal output, then surely the rest of our large organisational structures are only a few steps behind?

General Stanley McChrystal, who retired from the US Army as a four-star general after more than thirty-four years of service, wrote the bestseller *Team of Teams* in 2018.[xiii] It offers some mind-opening leadership philosophies, and the leverage of empathy for team performance is one of them. McChrystal covers a whole belief system that he honed in the army and has a particular focus on how to connect teams to work together and win together. Given his 'business context' was war zones, it is arguably quite surprising that empathy is a top takeaway from the book. As a backbone to his lessons however, McChrystal wholeheartedly believes that great leaders not only *show* empathy but encourage it in their teams. He comments that the best advice he ever got was from General John Zines, who emphasised the absolute need to understand the motivations and perspectives of others in order to succeed in battle. Once I had finished his book, I began researching the role of empathy in battle, and what I found was even more eye opening. I discovered that the formal requirement for empathy is deeply entrenched within the US Army leadership development toolkits. In the 2015 *US Army Handbook*, published online, there are twenty mandates surrounding the cultivation of empathy from soldiers.[xiv] Sections 6 to 9 state "*Leaders of character adhere to the Army Values, display empathy and the Warrior Ethos/Service Ethos*" and in the supporting training table alongside this they detail specifically what their expectations of the team are in this regard:

"Army leaders show empathy when they genuinely relate to another person's situation, motives, or feelings. Empathy does not mean sympathy for another, but a realization that leads to a deeper understanding. Empathy allows the leader to anticipate what others are experiencing and feeling and gives insight to how decisions or actions affect them. Leaders extend empathy to others in both their leader and follower roles. Leaders with a strong tendency for empathy can apply it to understand people at a deeper level."

If it is important enough for the army to recognise the importance of empathy when developing their teams to succeed in the most adverse scenarios, then it is certainly important enough for us to take note in the business world. From the President of the United States to one of the largest armies on the planet, the highest levels of leadership are acknowledging empathy's role in success. Given this, it is quite surprising how little we seem to have been talking about empathy on a day-to- day basis in our corporate lives and the media, but perhaps that is now beginning to change.

THE SCIENCE OF EMPATHY

I want to now turn to social science, psychology, and research studies to ensure that the practices in the chapters ahead are not only proven and relevant to business (and my personal experience of it), but also to the wider corporate, social, and academic worlds. Put simply, I want to assure you that it's not just me writing and talking about this but that there are plenty of people in other fields who are as passionate as I am. Some because it makes them feel more human, some because they are academics committed to this specialism, and some because they have seen it impact revenue, sales, customer service, or the people they have practised it with.

I had a moment in the autumn of 2019 that reiterated for me how important the inclusion of this 'academic' data would be. I had received a phone call from my mum, and the conversation went a bit like this:

MIMI: "Hi Mum, how are you?"

MUM: "Hi darling... you'll never guess what article I just read in the Sunday papers in the UK. Well, it was all about empathy and all those topics you've been talking about. I've cut it out for you and will scan it and email it to you tomorrow."

MIMI: "Thanks Mum, I really appreciate it and I can't wait to read it."

MUM: "Well I just thought 'what a coincidence' so I wanted to send it on right away..."

The fact that my mum, who is my biggest fan, believed at the time that this was a 'coincidence' was all the confirmation I needed.

If my mum still believed it might be just me on this whim to drive empathetic value for commercial wellbeing, versus a widespread professional and social issue, then I was bound to need to constantly prove my belief to a much wider circle. Incidentally, she did send me that article, and then a whole host of others from that moment on, because once you are aware of this theme and the increasing value of empathy and the people opening their eyes to it, you will spot it everywhere.

Fast forward six months to March 2020 and my mum and I had a second conversation about empathy. This time her takeaway was that "*I now don't seem to ever stop hearing about empathy on the radio*". Her insight was of course partly due to the COVID-19 social and health context of the time, and partly due to her heightened awareness of the topic, but it had become clear by 2020 that this deeply human theme was growing in gravitas and relevance daily. It was no longer a question of when leaders will take this on but at what pace. My prediction then was that 2020 would be the year when empathy went mainstream and it did. You will find it's not always written overtly as 'empathy'; it may be hidden in terms around 'connection', 'human values', 'people-led culture', 'active listening skills', 'compassion', 'corporate kindness', or 'conscientious leadership'. You name it and there will be some jargon, but fundamentally, they all lead toward the same theme of understanding others around you for pro- social corporate gain. The work for leadership now will be to entrench the need for empathy as a required set of skills within organisations across industries and management levels, but meanwhile, let's start with some facts.

In the United States, scientist Dr Tania Singer conducted an experiment all the way back in 2004 to track the brain's response to the pain of others. Her goal was to try and uncover an understanding specifically of how the brain works empathetically. Dr Singer and her team set out to prove that empathy has a firm and physical response in the brain that is capable of impacting decision and action. If you look her up, you'll see this is a journey she continues on today. The first experiment in Dr Singer's research unit involved a series of husband-and-wife couples and their ability to respond to pain inflicted on their partner, as a way to prove how (and if) we empathise with others around us. It doesn't sound at all pleasant, but basically what she did was attach a set of electrodes to each of the couples' hands and then deliver more painful or less painful electric shocks to them, while an fMRI scanner recorded their brain activity. Not the kind of test I would have enjoyed, but it did prove an incredibly valuable point. The test team ensured that just moments before each shock was administered, both members of the couple were able to see how strong the upcoming shock was going to be, and who would be receiving it. As the tests went on, it turned out that many of the same areas of the brain that are responsible for our own pain response lit up when their partner felt a shock, as well as when they themselves did. It showed that we have an ability to empathise, via neurons in our brains called mirror neurons, as a physical response in the brain when someone else is in pain. Whether they or their partner was feeling discomfort, their brains responded. Dr Singer's research proved that physically we can actually live or 'feel' the pain of others. Beyond this, the results also showed that the activation on the fMRI screen was even more intense for those who, in questionnaires given after the experiment, described themselves as "more empathetic".[xvi] The study showed the scientists enough evidence to suggest that empathy isn't simply 'feelings' or subjective response, it is indeed a functional reaction in the brain.

WHY BEING EMPATHETIC WORKS: EMOTIONAL CONTAGION?

The area of the brain responsible for empathy is the insular cortex, which is the part of the brain that connects information and emotions, as well as the area of grey matter where we experience physical pain. Much scientific research, using fMRI machines, has now suggested that when we empathise, we actually can 'feel' the same response as those we are responding to, but what more do we know?

We know that there are two forms of empathy: emotional empathy and cognitive empathy. Emotional empathy is the form that allows us to feel how another is feeling (to feel the same emotion), and cognitive empathy allows us to understand how another is feeling and take on their perspective. Emotional empathy is the form of empathy that happens automatically, without us needing to consciously focus on it. It is driven by mirror neurons in our brains that allow us to respond naturally to someone else's emotions in a similar way. These neurons are also responsible for making you yawn when you see someone else yawn. In fact, I would bet money on the fact that by the time you end this sentence about yawning, you will indeed have yawned. That's how powerful our mirror neurons are.

The discovery of mirror neurons has been one of the most important neuroscience discoveries of recent times, and it is these neurons that underpin our ability to naturally empathise with others. These neurons allow us to grasp the minds of others not through conceptual reasoning but through direct simulation: by feeling, not by thinking, or if we put this into a corporate context, by 'thinking with feeling'. Emotional empathy is the more primitive of the two forms of empathy and is much more subjective as it is the automatic response to how other people feel—sadness, excitement, fear or anxiety, etc.—and it is also the basis for sympathy and compassion. Some would argue that this form of empathy is a less needed set of skills in the corporate world, but I would argue that it is the ability to hone this form of empathy that can truly set a team or organisation apart.

The second form of empathy, cognitive empathy, is more deliberate. It activates the prefrontal cortex within the brain, which is where language is processed, and it is a triggered response with considered focus. Cognitive empathy is something that all leaders and teams can consciously hone; unlike emotional empathy, which happens 'to' us, cognitive empathy is a skill that can truly be nurtured within teams. The more we practise it the better we can use it.

WHY WE CHOOSE TO EMPATHISE

In 2011, researchers Jamil Zaki, an assistant professor of psychology at Stanford University, and Jason Mitchell, an associate professor of the social sciences at Harvard University, spent several years conducting neuroscience studies that attempted to link our innate emotional reward and responses to varying types of altruistic actions. Jamil Zaki has since released a book, *The War for Kindness: Building Empathy in a*

Fractured World, which is a fascinating read and reveals far more of the key findings that emerged across the various dimensions of empathy that they studied.[xvii] For brevity and in summary, their results began to unpack the synergy between empathy and our decision making surrounding generous behaviour. Their findings have provided evidence that empathy, as defined in their research through generosity and selflessness, is a deeply rooted part of who we are as a species. It is something we choose to do and something we enjoy.

In one of their studies, published in the *Proceedings of the National Academy of Sciences*, Zaki and Mitchell argue that, as people, we feel good when helping others, not because we are trying to avoid negative consequences or feel we have to, but because behaviours such as fairness, cooperation, and reciprocity are intrinsically rewarding to us.[xviii] We enjoy these emotions. The study alone could fuel the argument that given empathetic behaviour is fundamentally rewarding to humans, we could do worse than encourage this in our workplaces and business relationships. We know that when people feel good, they perform, they speak up, they act, and they are more open to trial or new ideas. Positive sentiment is directly linked to repeat behaviour and loyalty, so to me it's not a big leap to connect the Zaki and Mitchell research to a strong rationale for empathetic influence in the business environment as well as in marketing and innovation strategy.

There are further pieces of research that build on the findings above that suggest humans have an intrinsic, even intuitive, drive to help others. Several studies by Felix Warneken, of Harvard University, and Michael Tomasello of the Max Planck Institute in Germany, have both found that children as young as 18 months old spontaneously help people in need, for example, by opening a door for someone who has their hands full.[xix] The studies have shown that even young babies can look at a situation, empathise with the reality, and want to respond by helping or aiding the situation. Additionally, research by David Rand, of Yale University, along with Joshua Greene and Martin Nowak, also from Harvard, have found that when people are forced to make split-second decisions about whether to act kindly or in aid of people, they often choose to act kindly or selflessly.[xx] Ironically, it is only when people are given more time to consider their response that their self-interested instincts kick in!

"Kindness might be like psychological chocolate," says Zaki "...people might actually enjoy doing kind things for others, and that might be an emotional engine for driving pro-social behaviors."

Given our natural response seems to be an empathetic and emotional one (before an analytical or evidence-based one) it is wholly possible to strategically leverage this compelling and motivating approach to impact happiness and motivation in the workplace. People enjoy being kind because we are wired to care and to connect with those around us. The research suggests it and you don't have to look far to see this in action every day. Consider the guy who helps a stranger get down the stairs with multiple bags, the person who helps a new mum navigate the airport, or the people who work tirelessly for community charities in their spare time, often donating resources well beyond their own reach. There are examples of this behaviour all around us: we just have to sit back a moment to really take heed of its impact.

When we look at the behaviour of our communities and organisations around the world during and following the trauma of pandemics, crises, and natural disasters, these facets often appear naturally. When it comes down to it, being empathetic connected beings is both evolutionary, demanded, and motivating, and yet still we see so many examples of organisations not embodying this behaviour in the realms of corporate culture and leadership. It seems a strangely perverse, yet entirely socially accepted, parallel universe that we inhabit when the skills that are so naturally human disappear in the five-sevenths of our week when we identify ourselves as professionals.

'SOFT' SKILL OR POTENTLY POWERFUL CHANGE DRIVER?

I want to bring a further study in here that is perhaps even more revelatory. The study, 'Effects of Empathetic Communication in Healthcare Consultations', was published by the *Journal of the Royal Science of Medicine* in 2018.[xxi] The team in this case found, in a study across patients in six databases and a set of randomised trials in clinical settings, that when healthcare practitioners were trained to use empathetic communication with their patients before and during treatment, their patients actually experienced less pain! The study showed that empathetic communication between patients and practitioners sits at the very core of communicating in the healthcare and healing process—which seems pretty obvious when you read it here—and yet these results have remained in the healthcare world alone. Over the last two years of studying, I have often found that so much data that could be deeply impacting organisations remains in specialist fields, far from reaching its widest potential audience. This happens particularly in healthcare, education, and social work where the deep understanding of humanity and how we grow, motivate, and drive human behaviour and optimal learning could be having vastly wider impacts if we took the learnings into the business world. The results of this particular study mentioned here showed that doctors and nurses can be coached and trained in empathy, via a series of courses, in a way that improves patient responses in serious health issues over time. **It proves that empathy can be taught and learned,** and the results they saw didn't only enhance the quality of diagnosis and improve recovery, they also showed that the training resulted in fewer malpractice claims. In fact, the Cleveland Clinic in Ohio now has a staff unit and a podcast (called Studies on Empathy) that specifically talks about, and propagates, the learnings and lessons of the empathic specialists within the hospital.[xxii] There is a team of people dedicated to talking about how the change in mindset to one of empathy has resulted in multiple hospital improvement measures. In the conclusion of the study the researchers summarised:

"PRACTITIONERS WHO TAKE TIME TO ENHANCE HOW THEY EXPRESS EMPATHY AND DELIVER POSITIVE MESSAGES ARE LIKELY TO BRING SMALL IMPROVEMENTS TO A RANGE OF PSYCHOLOGICAL AND PHYSICAL PATIENT CONDITIONS, IMPROVE OVERALL PATIENT SATISFACTION WITH CARE."

JEREMY HOWICK, PHD, CLINICAL EPIDEMIOLOGIST AND PHILOSOPHER OF SCIENCE

"We found that conveying empathy and inducing positive expectations in healthcare consultations consistently reduced pain and anxiety by a small amount. Positive messages delivered by practitioners also seemed to improve some physical outcomes such as bronchial activity in asthmatic patients and physical function in postoperative patients. In the most common condition (pain), the effect of empathy and expectations interventions was equivalent to a 1- to 2-point reduction in pain on a 10-point visual analogue scale."

(Journal of The Royal Society of Medicine, 2015)[xxiii]

If the data is showing impact in the complex scientific and life-changing world of medicine, then surely we can make the smart assumption that in our own, much simpler, corporate and business world, empathetic communication can have a profound impact on how people feel and respond. It does seem like common sense when you start to consider that when people feel heard and listened to (whether it's your teenager, team member, or biggest client) they are more open, more engaged, more trusting, more loyal, and more motivated to respond. These are the basics of friendships, romantic relationships, and successful family dynamics. In the most simple and human form, when we feel understood we respond more positively. So, why is it that we are **undervaluing these facets in our business and professional relationships?**

The science paints a solid body of evidence, and there are many books dedicated to this topic alone. Dr Helen Riess's *The Empathy Effect* covers two hundred pages of neuroscientific analysis and results. *The Empathy Factor* by Marie R. Miyashiro offers two hundred more pages. Colombia University Press, *The Annual Review of Psychology,* University of Iowa, Oxford University Press, University of Chicago, and the list goes on. These are all institutions that have and are spending time and resources studying the neurodevelopment of empathy in humans. It is a body of writing that grows daily.

In writing this book I have tried to be empathetic to the 'leader reader' that I spot daily on their commute and in their daily grind. Those readers who are in an airport between flights, or reading around working schedules and email pings, and so I have kept the research succinct and easy to digest. There is much more out there but the majority of readers today have told me that they are easily distracted, surface- level absorbing, and looking for consumable intelligence without the weight. With that in mind, I have tried to provide enough to be convincing and concrete without cluttering your read with heavy cases and analysis.

At this point, I have unpacked much of the powerful evidence surrounding how critical and how fundamental empathy is to us as people. In the next chapter I want to start looking at the 'why'. Why did we evolve this way, and is empathy truly a facet of modern civilisation? In the chapter ahead, I turn to an African tribe of twelve million people, who still inhabit large parts of South Africa today: the Zulus, to explore these questions further.

Read on dear friend, and take a step back in time…

Chapter 4

THE ROOTS OF EMPATHY

It was easy for me to include evolutionary stories of empathy throughout this book, so deeply rooted a skill it is in our DNA as human beings. We can often understand a problem more deeply by looking back to how those before us behaved; the understanding of the role of empathy in modern society is no different. Looking back at the role empathy has played throughout human history is a window to its potential in our organisations—and indeed society—today. My favourite of these evolutionary examples derives from the point of view of the Zulu tribe, who date back many centuries to the early 1700s. The Zulu tribe's use of language and ancient cultural connection points, still in use today, wonderfully prove that we humans don't simply exist to survive, but to *thrive.* And beyond that, it is deeply embedded in our sense of self, as human beings, to know that we can *only* truly thrive as a group. The idea of thriving as a group is a theme that seems so often forgotten in our increasingly individualistic and solo society today, and one that is arguably right at the core of the Empathy Deficit growing in organisations all around us.

The Zulus' omnipresent and overt pro-social behaviour developed naturally over centuries to drive connection with each other as a critical part of their language and society. The common Zulu greeting when meeting another person is "*sawubona*" and rather than this meaning "*hello*", as many Western or other cultures tend to greet each other, it translates directly as "*I see you*" or more accurately "*I acknowledge your existence.*" A simple and powerful insinuation that the truest sense of connection and sense of reality beyond the physical person standing in front of you is to recognise the person and to see them. Don't we all want to be noticed and seen by those we take the time to greet? It is, after all, a pretty basic human need. To be seen. To be noticed. To know we matter.

The Zulu people are widely known for their practice and belief in a comprehensive empathetic everyday behaviour called 'ubuntu'. Ubuntu is a philosophy that influences daily decisions, behaviour, and the approach to relationships with families and friends. Widely adopted across South Africa today—and still taught in classrooms nationwide—it is hard to truly define but it can be understood as meaning 'humanity toward others' or reciprocity between people. It recognises the necessity of society to *understand* others. Ubuntu is founded on the need to look after the interests of others and to empathise with their needs when making decisions or choices. It is beautiful. It is a belief system we should teach every child and if it were ever practised truly on a global scale, it might have the power to change the world. Increasing numbers of academics and spiritual leaders around the world today agree with this fundamental South African understanding that, as humans, unlike most other species on Earth, we are *created to care and connect.* From one generation to the next we have rewired and refined our nervous systems, over and over again, to allow us to form a human blueprint that understands others around us and provokes pro-social behaviours that allow us to succeed. We have been honing empathy, and how we use it, for as long as we have existed, and it is at the core of our ability to run civilized societies—as well as successful businesses!

As a tribe that has survived rural Africa, war, and violent territorial challenges, the Zulu people's leverage of empathy is arguably a key facet in their strength and survival as a group. Incidentally, the response to the "*sawubona*" greeting is equally powerful in its empathetic influence: "*Ngikhona*" means *"I am here."* It is the perfect proof that we humans find the ultimate fulfilment in acknowledging being seen and valued by others. In knowing that you are not alone and that you are understood and connected to those around you.

"I see you.", "I am here." **Empathy in action at the deepest level.**

THE LEVERAGE OF EMPATHY IN LANGUAGE: "I FEEL YOU, MATE"

Bringing us back from the borders of Africa, do you recognise the phrases, "I feel you", or, "I feel your pain", often heard when two colleagues or friends are talking over a complex or uncomfortable situation?

Especially in the UK, where this is a widely heard phrase, this figure of speech is used without much thought, but when you start to unpack the meaning, you realise this is much more than simply a popular phrase; it is in fact an explanation of an innate human ability that we have honed over our two-hundred-thousand-year existence. Our survival and progress as a species have long stood on our ability to experience the reality or feelings of others; to empathise with them in order to protect and persevere as a group in challenging times.

For many decades, there has been a popular belief that human nature is fundamentally selfish (this has been propagated across pop culture, movies, and business culture) and that fundamentally we are out for ourselves above all else. As my own studies developed over the last few years, I began to believe that this viewpoint has much more to do with the organisational economics of past decades wanting us all to continue to believe the theory that benefitted them the most (making unending amounts of money per head), rather than actually having anything to do with our human nature. Today, I don't think for one moment that humanity is inherently self-centred. Our evolutionary behaviour has so often shown empathy to be a pro-social skill that we have leveraged to the benefit of our species across millennia, that it just doesn't feel possible that we were born to be self-centred above all else. Although social Darwinism (survival of the fittest) would have us believe we have to fight for ourselves above all else, to me this seems like a gross misunderstanding of human nature. Within both popular culture and management consultancy, the Darwinistic belief has become a self-fulfilling process that is gripping our organisations and societies globally, enforcing and cementing the opinion that it is in focusing on our ego and our distinctively competitive nature that we succeed. Yet, it is arguably not a valid principle of people, of human beings, when you look at how much of our motivation and our joy is tied to our connection to others. Think about the caveman era, when the ability to understand facial expressions or emotions could save someone else from eating a poisonous food or stop them from approaching a poor choice of partner. Simply by observing the facial expressions and body language of people in our own tribe, we guided and helped each other. We protected our strength as a team and ensured our survival day to day. Being able to empathise saved lives. It showed us what to avoid (driving personal survival) and when to help others in need (protecting the survival of the group). It connected us to our context.

ZULU:
"SAWUBONA"

ENGLISH:

"I ACKNOWLEDGE YOUR EXISTENCE."

In recent years we have well-evolved our use and leverage of empathy from life and death situations to everyday connections and relationships in our personal and business lives. Phrases such as "I feel you" now define themselves as not simply a metaphor but a neurologically significant response from the brain. Neuroscientists have proven that our brains have complex neurological 'mirrors' specifically placed to allow us to understand not just what someone else is thinking but also how they are feeling. It's a natural expression of our ability to understand others. To be able to walk in their shoes and see the world through their eyes. To empathise.

WHERE HAS ALL THE EMPATHY GONE AND WHY SHOULD I CARE?

In the last few decades, **we have found ourselves with worrying low levels of empathy, in a way that society has never witnessed before.** A study by the University of Michigan in 2010 analysed data on empathy among almost fourteen thousand college students over thirty years.[xxiv] The study found that kids in 2010 were 40 percent lower in empathy levels than their counterparts years before, with the last ten years seeing an increased speed of the decline. To further compound this imbalance, during this same period the levels of students' self-reported narcissism has reached new heights, according to research by Jean M. Twenge, a psychologist at San Diego State University. The research hasn't been repeated since, but one can assume this slide has continued, and much of the data to follow in later chapters of this book will support this assumption. As time has passed and we have become ever more urban, technologically connected, living alone, and geographically spread, we have been seeing the empathy drain from society.

The Empathy Deficit today is seen reflected in various social woes. We are experiencing the highest-ever rates of anxiety, low morale, low engagement, high staff turnover, and increasing levels of burnout and chronic stress-related illnesses. This is costing our governments hundreds of millions. Eighty- seven percent of people have no passion for their work, and over 40 percent of the US workforce has now

"TO TOUCH THE SOUL OF ANOTHER HUMAN BEING IS TO WALK ON HOLY GROUND."

STEPHEN R. COVEY, THE SEVEN HABITS OF HIGHLY SUCCESSFUL PEOPLE, 1992

chosen to be self-employed or work outside of corporate life. These figures are mirrored similarly in markets all over the world, so it's not a stretch to see that from a work-life standpoint, we are coming apart at the seams. Although science and a huge depth of research has proven that empathy is a skill that humans have relied and survived on as a species for hundreds of thousands of years, we seem to be letting this deficit continually grow without concerning ourselves about the consequences. You can't cut out a human trait that was built into our DNA and expect there to be no impact, and yet we seem to be doing just that.

Chapter 5

REGENERATING LEADERSHIP, REPOSITIONING GROWTH

In conversation with some of my elder, non- Millennial peers, in recent years, about the gap in empathy in industry many looked at me with a mix of disbelief and confusion. They told me that being 'kind' isn't a currency made for business growth and that the sharp edges we have embedded into our work are just a side effect of the digitisation of industry; the fourth revolution, or a deeper need to "make money not friends." Many of them see the capitalist edges as too ingrained for a principle of leadership that they see as 'soft', and they argue that there is no place for empathetic input in the workplace. (Somehow, they don't share these beliefs in their home life but cannot explain why.)

I always listen intently to their opinions and understand that for many leaders, trained in a previous era of leadership thinking, this move to more emotionally intelligent, empathetic influence and Regenerative Leadership is infinitely difficult to grasp. I also gently remind them, though, that when you have the same conversation with a Millennial leader, they understand intrinsically that this move isn't optional; it is what twenty- first-century business is already poised to be founded on.

In nearly all industry categories (from hospitality to medicine, travel to banking, insurance to plumbing), we are built on and by people. It should be a basic benchmark that leaders and CEOs see themselves as being there to sustainably serve their people and to do everything and anything they can to build and nourish the teams running and managing their industries. The leaders today who are embracing this concept are the leaders who are making waves and creating teams of loyal, fulfilled employees who stand the test of time: President Obama, Oprah, Simon Sinek (writer and thought leader), Jacinda Ardern (previous Prime Minister of New Zealand), Satya Nadella (CEO Microsoft), John Mackey (CEO Whole Foods). These are names you undoubtedly know, all well- known spokespeople and accomplished leaders who talk firmly to the role of empathetic influence and Regenerative Leadership as the future of our organisations and societies. It is fascinating to me that so few people seem to be listening because once you think about the stance of these visionary leaders, it seems basic common sense. Listen to people, understand them, put them first, and then reflect this in your leadership and your working environment, allowing them to thrive. Not rocket science.

So why, if it is both obvious and genetically rendered into our DNA, are so many organisations around the world today simply not getting this right? And why aren't more leaders considering this overt threat to empathy as a direct threat to their businesses?

REGENERATING BUSINESS, REGENERATIVE LEADERSHIP

The emotional barrier, lack of experience, or basic fear surrounding a move into Regenerative Leadership is part of the answer. A transformation journey that feels all too natural to me and many of my Millennial cohorts, supported by a very compelling and credible data set, is often too far removed from the legacy training and experience sets of many of today's leaders. Theirs is a different era with a different set of data, life lessons, and mentors. They haven't been trained this

"THROUGH EMPATHY BUSINESSES ARE MORE LIKELY TO THRIVE."

HELEN RIESS, M.D., ASSOCIATE CLINICAL PROFESSOR OF PSYCHIATRY, HARVARD MEDICAL SCHOOL

way, they haven't seen the world react this way, they didn't move through businesses that were run this way. They cannot work out how to start acting in this way. For them, businesses are not something they can see as regenerative (cyclical, sustainable, and ever improving) but 'generative': entities that generate growth and profit and continue to create increasing output within a linear system.

Perhaps these leaders are too busy focusing on profit margin to consider the margin of error that they are experiencing by not looking at each of their teams in their individual contexts? Or perhaps we can blame the many MBA programs around the world for acurriculum that has assumed business success is directly related to shareholder profit and is based only on case studies from eras gone by? Personally, I suspect the overriding reason is that these leaders simply have never been taught anything like this way of thinking. They have honed their leadership style based on their predecessors who formulated their approach in the boom years of growth in the 1970s and 1980s. Years where the focus was on money and business growth and not much else. A time when leaders had more interest in shareholder value than the value of the people who were creating and consuming those very same shareholder dollars.

Whether you like it or loathe it, the businesses of these times were booming. Arguably they had a solid reason for why they weren't focusing on anything remotely regenerative (they didn't need to regenerate; they were busy generating 'more' on an unprecedented scale!), but either way this 'growth above all else' has had a lasting impact that is causing deeply negative ripples on the workforce all these years later. Organisational culture at large has found it very hard to move on from this mindset.

You only have to look at the business language of that time to see how deeply this 'business above all else' mindset was:

"Crush the competition" "Time is money"
"Kill it"
"Set it in stone" "Human resources"
"Organisations are machines" "Growth at all costs"
"Give 'em hell"

DECADES OF DECADENCE AND THE LEADERSHIP HANGOVER WE ARE HANDLING

Here's the thing though: It's not the '80s anymore. Millennials and Gen Z's want to love their jobs and they want to love them holistically in a way that creates meaning for them. They believe in regenerative life at home and at work. The idea of simply consuming, creating more, and consuming again feels anciently out of fashion and out of favour. Millennials want to love their jobs because they feel proud that they chose this job over any other, because they choose to spend their time there, and because they are not willing to spend ninety thousand hours over a lifetime doing something they don't love. It's always about more than just money for them. The macro context that they are living in is already so full on, so full of uncontrollable anguish and tension, that they assume that their workplace, something that they can control, shouldn't be. They want to understand the bigger picture because it reflects their own.

This generation is younger, with less scepticism or bad experiences to influence their opinions. We are not afraid of change, big ideas, or saying what we think, and we are not afraid of demanding to 'love' what we do. This younger workforce defines growth in an entirely different way and I see it around me all the time. Growth for us means many things: It means not standing still; it means learning, inventing, and inspiring; it means constantly evolving, but very rarely does it equate to financial growth or linear production alone. According to LinkedIn's Workplace Culture Report in 2018, nearly nine out of ten (86 percent) Millennials would consider taking a pay cut to work at a company whose mission and values better aligned with their own. By comparison, their older bosses felt very differently, with only 9 percent of those between the ages of fifty-four and seventy-two agreeing.[xvii]

The Millennial group knows that they are the future of the organisations and they want to know what their purpose is for being so. It can't simply be to continue growing the company. That is like a foreign language to us. It doesn't mean anything, it doesn't have purpose beyond its output. We need to know why we would and should commit, and what we will be adding to the world, to society, to our customers by doing so. For a very long time the business world has been failing to deliver this answer to us. It seems to me that whilst so many industries have their purpose clearly mapped out—teachers teach to elevate their students, architects design to advance our cities, lawyers practice to bring about a safe and fair society—it is only 'business' at large that seems to exist purely to make money. When you look at it like this it is a mind-boggling concept. It is true that making money makes the world go around, but it is also true that business shouldn't be able to damage, or continually 'take' from its people, without simultaneously regenerating its context as it makes more money.

Millennials feel like there are endless options open to us. Probably because there are. This means we can afford to be choosy and only do the things we love and that therefore make us happy. We believe in feeling joy. If we find a business that shares our ideals and allows us to flourish (not just within the company but also within our lives) we are a pretty loyal bunch, but from the moment we feel as though the leader we look up to has not got our back or doesn't recognise or understand us, we back off. Sadly, ours is an age defined by distrust, anxiety, loneliness, and fear and therefore paying acute attention to what this means to us, the workforce, is important. Millennials are often said to be an 'entitled' group. As a sweeping statement it is probably accurate in many ways. But much deeper and of more relevance is that this group is entirely intolerant of anything that exploits their shared beliefs for self-expression and identity, or for their own future visions. They are an entire generation brought up to be this way. They want to be connected to something bigger than themselves and they will fight for it—for them, for their network, and for their planet. Their solidarity to this is both unending and contagious. The need to be connected to a greater whole and a purpose, to feel we are part of a valuable story and greater good, is deeply embedded into our being. We need to be seen and feel heard, and as the turmoil of the world gets ever faster and deeper, our need to know we have a place that is connected to our own unique identity, and also that of the group, is paramount.

"...THE NARRATIVE THAT BUSINESS IS ALL ABOUT MONEY AND PROFIT IS JUST FUNDAMENTALLY WRONG. IT'S DOING GREAT DAMAGE TO THE WORLD, ACTUALLY, BECAUSE IF BUSINESS IS NOT ALLOWED TO CREATE HOLISTIC VALUE (BECAUSE IT'S FUNDAMENTALLY SELFISH, GREEDY, AND IT'S A SOCIOPATHIC INSTITUTION), THEN OUR WORLD IS NOT GOING TO FULLY ESCAPE FROM POVERTY AND PROSPERITY. IT'S GOING TO REVERSE."

JOHN MACKEY, AUTHOR OF CONSCIOUS CAPITALISM

Something that until now, capitalist society and the corporate world has not yet created enough space for.

In all honesty, Millennials are not that different from our ancient ancestors. For a long time, all of humanity was constantly fearing extinction, and that meant that connecting to each other was a survival mechanism. For Millennials it's not so different, it's just that 'survival' is now less about outrunning a sabre-toothed tiger and more about maintaining group-think status to protect our beliefs and shared purpose or goal. Our ancestral beliefs surrounding group connectivity and understanding have been embedded into our beings and culture to drive our decision making; we can't help it. Today we fight for our opinions a little harder and louder (and often on a social platform to an audience of millions), and occasionally we can be obtuse in doing so, but fundamentally, the approach to maintaining the balance of the wider group around us remains intact. This isn't new news.

As a small example of how impactful even a small disconnect with a Gen X/Boomer leader can be for the new generation running our organisations today, I am reminded of an occasion when I was attending a global leadership conference in Europe a couple of years ago. I was sitting in a room of fifty or so senior leaders from across the world, fighting off extreme jet lag and where I was in the minority as a female under forty (in fact, I was probably the only one.) It was, however, nothing to do with the demographic that creates a story of millennial disconnect here, but something the senior leader in the room said without realising its impact that instantly created an empathetic gap between us. On giving the opening speech of the day, the leader in question mentioned a few of the leaders in the room and their particular successes in their markets around the world. Given I was one of those highlighted, that should have been enough to make the long-haul flight there entirely worthwhile. Instead, however, in the same sentence the leader moved on to one, killer, *incorrect* fact. A fact that undermined everything I had fought for following what had been a particularly arduous yet successful project. In one sentence the leader inadvertently took away a deep commitment to a client that I had loved back to health, and that until that moment had been ticking all the Millennial must-have boxes nicely.

So, what did the leader say?

In the opening speech and introduction, the leader underestimated my time in the company pretty significantly. Not by a month of two, no, by an entire year, 365 days of my life that I would never get back and that the leader had seemingly not even noticed that I, and my team, had been around for. In that fleeting moment, in front of an entire room of people, the leader showed me that we were of so little value to her bigger picture that she could underestimate the commitment by twelve long months. Today, the workforce is in it for the 'why'—the purpose, the meaning—and in that under-representation, the person at the very top created not just an empathetic gap between us but a canyon-size disconnect. If empathy is about understanding others and being able to see the world through the eyes of those who work for us, these kinds of mistakes are monumental. A simple slip or lack of focus can lead to a devaluation of a key team member in one sweeping statement.

Those few words not only wiped away any shared human values or empathetic understanding (of what the effort and commitment meant to those that led it) but also erased a percentage of the business value that I would be able to commit to the brand going forward. Fundamentally, this empathy gap wiped dollar signs off the bottom line: an empathetic deficit that directly drove a financial deficit. The instant demotivation was not only a personal feeling but also had an immediate impact on the resources I had previously been openly committing. After all, if the human value is so 'undervalued' when compared to the financial value of the results, the input no longer seems worthwhile.

When you consider leadership that falls within regenerative and empathetic practices, those that fall short become what I would term a detached leader. Detached Leadership is a term I coined to describe leaders who constantly create a gap empathetically or emotionally between themselves and their team members, and who are categorically not creating a *ripple* beyond their own office doors. These senior level people are working in isolation from their teams or at least from parts of their teams.

It is no simple feat to connect with an entire organisation, but there are those who manage it seamlessly. Leaders who go to lengths to remember the details and the data that are important to those in their charge. I once read about the former CEO of Cisco Systems, John Chambers, and his commitment to always calling staff personally upon discovering they had experienced a personal loss. It was his policy that within forty-eight hours he would call them and offer help and support. That has stuck with me always and of course it sticks with their employees, too. Cisco Systems has consistently been rated as one of the best places to work in the USA, with a culture of connectivity and compassion that consistently puts people at the top of the agenda.[xxviii]

Back in the meeting room in Europe, I don't think I heard the rest of the speech that day, and it becomes a perfect example of how being unable to stand in someone else's shoes can create striking disconnects in corporate culture and motivation. I suspect there are plenty of older, Gen X/Boomer leaders out there reading this tale saying *"oh just deal with it, she was your boss."* But these things matter to Millennials. The truth is that I don't need to 'deal with it' or 'get over it' because in today's extremely small global world, three things are critical to consider. First, our jobs are our lives so getting it right at work matters. Second, the world is wide open, so once a leader has proven overtly that they are entirely disconnected with the shoes their team members walk in every day, the gap is already formed. Third, in a faster-paced, erratic, and more complex business environment than ever before, the need to work together closely and collaborate fluidly is a prerequisite to compete and stay ahead.

Essentially, businesses should be able to regenerate their people, the planet, and the wellbeing of those committed to driving their success. The workplace Empathy Gap is increasingly at risk of continuing to grow for businesses that don't recognise that this new crew—the Millennials— are in town and in your organisation. They are facing your clients and customers every day. They are running the business relationships already, and the future really is theirs to shape.

Best we start to close that gap pretty fast, right?

"FILMMAKERS CAN TURN THEIR CAMERAS TO CAPTURE SHARED HUMAN QUALITIES AND BREAK STEREOTYPES OF VARIOUS NATIONALITIES AND RELIGIONS. THEY CREATE EMPATHY BETWEEN US AND OTHERS. AN EMPATHY WE NEED TODAY MORE THAN EVER."

ASGHAR FARHADI, ACADEMY AWARD–WINNING FILM DIRECTOR, 2017

Chapter 6

IS CAPITALISM THE ENEMY?

In recent years it has become clear that the capitalist thinking that forms the basis of our business theory today is often entirely in opposition to the things that allow us to thrive as people: true connectivity, inspired creativity, personal identity, and recognition, all dwindling under ever-tighter organisational pressure. These relationship-based facets take time to nurture, foster, and encourage. They are human-led interventions that take emotional intelligence to navigate and bottom line–driven thinking often doesn't allow the time or investment necessary. So, is capitalism behind the decline of empathy levels? Not alone perhaps but absolutely in part.

The Empathy Deficit took hold of organisation culture in the early 2000s while we were all looking the other way (toward the dollar signs!) While we were altogether too busy focusing on improving margin and elevating the bottom line, we lost each other. As the world became driven by higher targets, smaller budgets, and tighter timelines, the facets that originally allowed our industries and our people to thrive—creativity, human connection, and engagement—have been under intense fire. We have become the machine instead of the spark, and whilst machines can run on autopilot in a systematic 'action and repeat' format, inspired humans can't. During this ongoing 'machine-isation' of our output, ideas, and processes there has been very little room for anything that could look like empathy, conscientious connection, or human reciprocity. We are too busy, working too many hours without enough rest, to ever think about anything other than the next email, promotion, or profit structure. We have stopped using our energy and creativity to consider what those working alongside us want and need to equally thrive, and it's therefore no wonder that the under-forties are looking around and questioning what on earth the value of their day job is. Has capitalism truly been blocking our ability to lead as *people* above all else? Can a for-profit organisation be a source of elevation in all areas of our lives, serving every stakeholder equally, most notably the employees, and not just the shareholders?

The answer to both questions is yes, but there has to be a conscious shift to making it so.

"LEADERSHIP IS ABOUT EMPATHY."

OPRAH WINFREY

THE STATUS QUO

Many leaders today believe that their key role is to be 'in charge' of the business, single-mindedly driving the highest return to their shareholders, but I disagree. Of course, there are critical financial output measures, and I am not suggesting for a moment that businesses shouldn't be profitable, but the responsibility of the CEO is to the people who look after their business and how those people underpin the numbers. It is a turn of the current unilateral focus on 'looking after the numbers' to a more multidimensional view of an organisation, starting with the people on the line every day. This is not about replacing money-making but about a new methodology as to how we make money. You only have to look at Microsoft CEO Satya Nadella, a deep believer in an empathetic mantra to drive business change, to see how this can come to life. Satya has been heralded for fusing people-led culture with the brand's turnaround, and won *Financial Times* Person of the Year in 2019 for his success in doing so, returning over one trillion dollars to shareholders in his six-year tenure. In his book, *Hit Refresh,* Satya notes that his highest priority is renewing the company culture with a growing sense of empathy. The word 'empathy' appears over fifty times throughout the book and across nearly every article or video featuring the global CEO today.[xxix]

"PEOPLE WITHOUT SOCIAL EMOTIONS LIKE EMPATHY ARE NOT OBJECTIVE DECISION MAKERS. THEY ARE SOCIOPATHS."

DAVID BROOKS,
CULTURAL COMMENTATOR,
IN THE NEW YORK TIMES, *2009*

THE PEOPLE'S LEADER

So, what might this mean to a wider set of organisations?

When leaders lack empathy, and place value entirely on the data and results without truly understanding the path to getting there, they can lose the potential to inspire and build monumentally greater success. I recently heard Simon Sinek say that leaders often think they are in charge of their organisations, but that in his opinion they are not and that instead they should be responsible for those *in their charge.*[xxx] He argues firmly that when a CEO states their number one priority is their 'customer', they are looking in the wrong direction. When capitalist leaders build a business that is creating value beyond the cost of their resources, they see themselves as prospering. They define this as success. But the truth is, you can only truly succeed if you have an understanding and respect for those who are driving the creation of that value for you.

The global businesses leading in this way today, businesses such as Whole Foods, Microsoft, and Southwest Airlines, know this to be true.

They drive this belief deep into their cultural and operational DNA. It's that simple. They understand that with a deeper understanding of their people they can overcome the barriers, the anxiety, the tension, and the cultural gaps of large companies, and that magically people begin to 'heal'. Confidence goes up, creativity goes up, productivity goes up. People talk more, strategies develop further, and hey presto, business begins to turn. It is the magic formula that really contains very little magic. Today we simply cannot defend business success solely on the back of self-interest. The decade ahead of us is for those who embrace shared understanding and connectivity as the most prized and profitable path to shared accomplishments.

GOING BACK TO THE BEGINNING

Commerce hasn't always been like it is today. If you look back at the beginnings of commercial transactions, business began between two people working together for mutual gain. Both parties knew that to be connected and to treat each other with respect was not only good for business, and repeat business, but it was also a foundation for human engagement and decency. We valued this care and understanding greatly in growing and driving successful ventures. But then we forgot. In the wave of dollars that flew into our bank accounts and fast cars that drove into our driveways, we focused on money and humanity moved down our lists. Strange, seeing as it was our own people we were deprioritising, but true.

Many generations since have lost the knack of true relationship building due to a global culture of independence rather than interdependence. Our society has been pushed ever further apart by social media and a robot-interrupted age as well as the frequency of solo living and urban isolation. Whether it is a sustainable, planet-changing cause or simply a valuable business network of people, when the connection is cut to the things that Millennials and Gen Z's value, the resulting problems span from demotivation and low output to a host of wider-reaching social and professional impacts such as self-isolation, low confidence, and underperformance. Inclusivity, recognition, and tolerance of our opinions is not just a preference, it is a requirement and fuels our natural desire to group, whether socially online or IRL (in real life), with those who empathise with our own outlook.

Regenerative leaders today acknowledge that times have changed for good, and that the things the workforce need you to recognise and empathise with are as critical as the money you pay them. Employees want you to recognise their emotional value, their personal commitment, **their soul as well as their role.** The idea of a job for life, or even for five years, has flown out of the window and risk taking is actively encouraged across the board, so once you have lost a team member, there is very little chance to bring them back.

In the end, if we lose out on empathic connection, we lose out on the people protecting the shareholder value we all so dearly desire.

Chapter 7

THE IMPACT OF AN INCREASINGLY DETACHED WORLD

Gone are the days when we grew up, worked, got married, had our kids, and got old in the same village or town we were born in. That was our universe and we were happy with it. We didn't know anything else and we didn't demand happiness beyond what we were given. We accepted it and we found happiness within it.

Many of us today would look at that traditional reality and say "*how dull*", but there was an intrinsic safety and comfort in that reality. We felt secure; we knew the playing cards and we knew what to expect day in and day out. The bottom of Maslow's Hierarchy of Needs was firmly entrenched and our grounding was firm. Our expectations were managed and people knew us, our stories, and our families. The community around us understood our context and where we were coming from, literally and figuratively. There was empathy oozing from every community meeting, town centre parade, or corner pub due to our shared context and history. We were a community above all else.

THE POWER OF COMMUNITY

Many definitions of community explain the term along the lines of "*the condition of sharing attitudes and interests in common.*"[xxxi] **It turns out therefore that the definition of community is not so different from the definition of empathy**. Fundamentally, when we were living in consistent close-knit communities and we were consistently connected, we thrived. Perhaps not in today's corporate definition of thriving, not in a reaching the top, career-growth kind of way, but we grew solidly over time, arguably in the way humanity intended. We weren't as *out of sorts* as we are now and we certainly didn't struggle with the levels of anxiety, corporate burnout, loneliness, or depression that we see today. Looking back at those times we can learn a little about our need to feel connected. When we surround ourselves with the deep bonds of friendship and camaraderie with those who walk the same path we do, we heal emotionally, our children learn faster, our elderly live longer, and our happiness levels soar. We are social beings and whilst our context has changed, our humanity hasn't.

We very rarely have the same sense of safety today that we once did in those 'home' communities and we are missing so many fundamental, reliable, day in and day out needs because of it. The safety 'criteria' that Maslow put at the base of his pyramid (as an essential requirement for success) is so often missing, and I would argue that we are unhappy because of it. When our needs for emotional and physical safety are not met, it is very difficult for us to focus on the higher order needs or self-actualisation (growth, confidence, inspiration), which tend to be the needs that facilitate empathising with others effectively. High stress is empathy's greatest enemy.

These critical safety foundations however, are often only highlighted when we see great shifts or even tragedy in society. At other times we are far too busy running fast and consuming faster. In mid-2020, as the COVID-19 virus spread around the world, however, the global community acknowledged that although the fiscal fallout of the corona pandemic was bound to be enormous, empathising with the more imminent health and isolation crises faced by the broader community was the first point on every agenda. Empathy suddenly became a word that the media and every social media platform drove forward as there was a mass need to connect with those around us, all the while being physically apart.

However, the majority of our jobs are nowhere near offering the replacement of the village culture we evolved to thrive within. We now spend most of our time with a group of people in a shared physical environment yet barely connecting beyond the project we share or the lunch break we happen to cross over in. This is a societal issue with far- reaching effects and Detached Leadership is responsible for much of it. If you are the *village* chief, it is your role to pull the *village* together, to create the ripple, and to ensure that neither you nor your team are detached within the corporate community you are leading. More often than not, however, it seems the leaders have missed this memo entirely.

THE IMPACT OF DETACHMENT ON OUR HEALTH AND LIVES

In 2010, an academic meta-analysis study suggested that the influence of disconnected social relationships on the risk of premature death might be comparable to the much more well-established risk factors to mortality such as smoking and alcohol consumption.[xxxii] Amazingly, the risks suggested in the research exceeded the risk of many more common threat factors such as obesity or physical inactivity. It makes me wonder how we are not taking this more seriously in the workplace!

As the quality and quantity of our social relationships is flowing ever downward in the working environments we spend so much time in, we have a scarily accurate set of trends predicting lower levels of health and wellbeing. Today we see less intergenerational living, greater social and professional mobility, higher numbers of dual-career families, and an increased number of single households. All these factors point to the fact that outside of the working environment, our team members are ever more likely to be alone or isolated, so surely it follows that we should be working harder to connect to each other in the environments we share.

In the same study mentioned above, which uses data across 308,849 individuals over an average of 7.5 years, the results indicated that individuals with adequate social relationships have a 50 percent greater likelihood of survival compared to those with poor or insufficient social relationships. This creates an amazingly compelling case for not being alone and lonely! The report also references the study of high mortality rates, many decades ago, among infants in custodial care (i.e. orphanages) when those children spent many hours a day alone, even when controlling for pre-existing health conditions and medical treatment.[xxxiii] Lack of human contact was proven to predict mortality, and medical professionals at the time were stunned to learn that infants would die without social interaction. This single finding, so simple in hindsight, was responsible for changes in practice and policy that markedly decreased mortality rates in custodial care settings. Yet what is amazing is that this data never enters the corporate world. So often, healthcare or educational research is stuck in segregated industries and the business community misses out on this intelligence. We could be reaching and impacting so many more people through the direct channels we have with them, and yet we are not. Five-sevenths of our weeks are spent at work, which means that business leaders and brands have enormous power to change society from the inside (of organisations) out, should they choose to positively activate it. And we employees? We want them to! If you look at the most successful videos, ads, and films, the ones that truly make a mark and 'go viral', they are more often than not ones that show humanity in its most natural and connected form. They offer a reflection of true human nature and an accurate reflection of our most deep-rooted ideals and needs. The reality is that we want this from our leaders as well as our screens! If only we could convince more leaders of the power of these mutually cohesive connection points. As with films and content, when we are able to create a bond with our co-workers, we foster a desire to move forward together.

What all this evidence points to is that when we are out of sync with our villages, we are out of sync both physically and emotionally across all areas of our lives. If we are not surrounded by empathetic engagement on a consistent basis, we can die younger, have more heart attacks, recover less quickly, and cognitively develop more slowly. In fact, based on the research, empathising and connecting with each other is not only about enhancing our quality of life, it is also about survival. The data suggests that the medical relevance of social relationships in wellbeing is well established, and it's therefore no longer an 'if' but a fact that we evolved to thrive together.[xxxiv] Despite social media and technological advancements to connect us via chat apps, video calls, and Facebook groups, people are increasingly remote, and this should concern us. As leaders today and of the future, it's time to intervene.

CLIMBING UP AND CONNECTING LESS

As an advertising agency director, I have the privilege of seeing the inside, being on the inside, of multiple clients' offices across industries every week. The detachment I see between the 'top' and the 'middle' is remarkable. The leaders at the top separate themselves in closed-off areas and 'exec meeting rooms', and the teams in the 'middle' wander past those very same rooms with indifference and anxiety in a balanced tango. Neither side really understands the agenda or the motivations of the teams they work with, and although the 'village' chiefs may hold respect, they also create a reprise of distanced and often suboptimal commentary in the corridors and emails. Nobody truly knows who they are! People know their title and their name and possibly their vision, but there is no personal engagement with that leader as a fellow human with a shared goal. This means that surely neither the leader nor the team members can possibly achieve their full potential? I often feel like dropping a note under the 'exec' meeting room door with the simple message: "Ninety-three percent of employees say they're more likely to stay with an empathetic employer. Step outside your boardroom, walk to the kitchen and listen to your team."[xxxv] I haven't yet but maybe one day I will!

These leaders can't placate their teams with words or visionary statements because the reality is that their teams want authentic, tangible change. It's not about words or corporate policy; it's about heartfelt, value-adding, life- enhancing action that responds to the intended group, and not to a handbook designed for 'global brand standards' or tailored to a 'worldwide HR policy'. It should be action that connects people with people and talks directly to the teams they manage. In the end, the detachment doesn't create the respect that is intended but instead creates a void that stops the flow of authenticity between fellow humans sharing a workplace. This detachment has for so long been seen as a standard practice of business hierarchy, and even as businesses became flatter, more modern structures with open plan offices and shared all-company meetings, those at the top still believe the gap, the detachment, is a motivating segregation. Something to aspire to. Something to be proud of. This is most likely a shadow cast by many previous generations of command and control, but within the information age, this couldn't be more counterintuitive or irrelevant.

Many years ago, Adam Galinsky, Fellow at Colombia University, completed a study to test a hypothesis that once people start to feel powerful, their ability to see things from another's perspective deteriorates.[xxxvi] His research concluded that indeed the people who perceive themselves to be in positions of power are less likely to judge the social experience of others accurately. It is therefore the leaders who practise empathy and understanding that stand out and drive exceptional performance from their people. If the majority of today's leaders are naturally less empathetic, then surely that is a rallying cry for the ones who want to create change to purposely focus on being otherwise?

Empathy is not such a 'soft' skill once you realise it is a powerful differentiator from the competition. Further research by APS Fellow Michael Inzlicht of the University of Toronto supported Galinsky's findings when he looked at empathetic functioning in the brain and discovered that the study participants who were primed to feel more powerful had dampened empathetic activity in their brain.[xxxvii] It is an issue that we can now be acutely aware of; moving up the proverbial ladder can weaken the empathetic skills of those climbing fastest.

THEORY OF MOTIVATION

The talk about flexi time, extended parental leave, or open plan entertainment areas as solutions for workplace disconnect is deeply flawed in my opinion. These benefits are simply the corporate world's version of palliative care, necessary but not revolutionary. They might allow teams to temporarily mask the symptoms of a much deeper set of cultural, lifestyle, or working issues, but they won't create sustainable motivation or reward. Although commendable, these benefits are not addressing the empathetic void; they are simply copycat mechanisms that the media drive as a new benchmark in modern business. They show no true understanding of one organisation's team needs over another, and certainly they do not connect to empathetic engagement with a team of people. They may connect people to the basics of work-life integration, but they don't connect them to the leadership team that signed them off. Putting in a pool table and free healthy snacks is not going to address the depth of this human need, and neither is circulating an email about 'mental health awareness' days. These band-aid interventions entirely miss out on empathising with the actual problem. There is a great power in the specifics of environment to address issues associated with isolated or non-functioning workplaces, but it cannot be a solution unto itself; it is part of a larger puzzle. Very soon these benchmarks will be commonplace and expected by every

Millennial and Gen Z that walks in the door of any given organisation. They absolutely do not make your company different or less likely to lose your best people.

It is the Millennials themselves who have already started to enforce better working engagements, heathier living, and a focus on sustainability. These agendas are based on their own empathy for others and their innate human desire to connect with the people, places, and planet around them. As these Millennials get into more and more senior positions with louder voices and impact, the C-suite leadership will have to embrace this approach as a need-state and not an optional extra. For these younger guys now running brands and businesses, changing corporate structures and removing the ice-cold Detached Leadership cultures of old and transforming them into structures and cultures that represent real people with their real lives is expected and natural. Indeed, this generation is more in touch with their natural instinct as to how to lead than any that came before them. We are going back to the future. Literally.

RECONNECTING THE DOTS

Various people have asked me whether 'empathy' in industry is something we have lost over time, or whether it was never really there. I don't think the answer is clear cut as it varies from country to country, industry to industry, and brand to brand, but what I do think is clear is that the corporate landscape is now more complex, disconnected, and fragmented than ever before, from both a talent and an audience point of view, and regardless of whether this means we lost our empathetic compass or never had it, we now need an entirely different depth of empathy in business.

Today, and in the post COVID-19 era, we need to go up a notch—a serious, Olympic high jump–level notch. Perhaps the Empathy Deficit has been caused by less time and higher pressure, fewer full lunch hours and more late nights, but somehow along the way we have become far too mechanical about the ways we lead and connect with those around us, and no longer will the workforce accept this. It is not motivating or regenerating, and it is certainly not sustainable.

The lack of human connectivity is not just impacting the workplace, or the motivation of teams to stick around, it is impacting our whole lives. The disconnect people feel from their leaders and fellow teams, and the corporate pressure they feel they are sinking under, makes for an altogether less enjoyable, balanced, or healthy lifestyle. In fact, it's dangerously impacting our personal lives. According to a 2018 survey, more than two in ten adults in the USA and the United Kingdom now say they "always" or "often" feel lonely, alone, isolated or left out[4].[xxxviii] Work cannot only be to blame, but however you look at it, we have a problem and it's a wide-reaching one.

Loneliness has now become endemic across the world, and we have to face the fact that as businesspeople and business leaders, today or of the future, we are part of the cause.

Chapter 8

LONELY BUT

NOT ALONE

It is often said that it is lonely at the top, but loneliness at work is a far wider-reaching issue than for those in the C-suite offices alone. While our populations boom, our lack of connectedness results in a similarly fast-growing lack of contentedness that bellows loudly that we have never been lonelier. We fly from one role to the next, crossing cities, countries, and international borders on our journey to professional growth and higher salaries, but we don't have the ability to take our tribe—our *village*—the people who really know us, with us. We therefore lose the *village* we once thrived in and we replace it with an open-plan selection of 'colleagues' who share our passion for coffee and a good joke, but there it ends.

I have lived on five continents surrounded by a wider set of colleagues than I could ever have hoped for. I have met some of the most inspiring and fantastically engaging people on all corners of the planet, from insight specialists in Malaysia to township marketing specialists in South Africa to experts in Arab traditions in the United Arab Emirates. Although I don't plan on stopping this journey through the world's wonders any time soon, I am very aware of the fact that it is deeply unsettling to constantly surround yourself with people you have no legacy with, even if you do love what you are doing. As businesspeople today, we are a disconnected group, detached in our search for work and corporate communities that we hope we will love, wherever we land, yet the reality is that, more often than not, we fly through this business world alone.

Of course, this 'alone-ness' is not always in the *physical* sense. We are often surrounded by more people, from more corners of the world, than ever before, but we are 'alone' in the sense that we are alone in our journey and our context; we are socially alone. We are alone, together. We set a path for career success or a new job, and every time we make a change we begin again as a lone ranger among a constantly moving group of fellow passionately skilled colleagues, who are ultimately total strangers to us and our history. As teams, we don't often share experience, lifestyle, context, or even a 'home' language with those standing right next to us, sharing our desk, or working within our units. We don't know each other very well at all, and that makes us uncomfortable and lonely, albeit subconsciously. We may not know why we have this slightly discontented feeling, this 'gut feel' that something is not quite as it needs to be, but it lingers with us. It is heavy and it can be sad. These are feelings that track all the way back to historical times when we needed others to physically survive and therefore loneliness was a perceived threat to our survival. Feeling alone, or community-less, is against our intrinsic human nature and we don't enjoy it one bit.

Today, this perceived risk is a potent mix of emotional and physiological discomfort. Doctors and researchers are looking ever more deeply into the effect of stress, and loneliness and anxiety, as a direct *physical* impact, as well as facets that affect our mental health.[xxxix] From eroding the immune system to impacting brain functionality, those suffering with severe loneliness have been seen to suffer from an array of physical illnesses. Under intense pressure, the human body responds by focusing on bacterial infections and reduces its production of virus-fighting abilities. Not good news for a global population fighting a flu pandemic. The long-term impacts can also see those who are socially isolated over time suffer from higher rates of cancer, infection, heart disease, and even premature mortality.[xl] As our consistent stress levels rise and the hormone cortisol increases steadily in our bodies, we see greater numbers of heart attacks and strokes, and this is before factoring in the mental and emotional health of the patient. Loneliness can be a very dangerous condition. When we see it increasing on a global scale, at such speed, it becomes very apparent that we have a physical health crisis, as well as a mental health crisis, on our hands,[xli] and it's not something we should be standing by to watch from the sidelines.

THE JOURNEY TO LONELINESS

We may hide the effects, push them aside or ignore them entirely, but then one evening at home it will sneak up on us as a gaping hole that we had been suppressing in our day-to-day life. It follows that the more uncomfortable and stressed we become, the harder it is for us to connect or empathise with those around us, and the Empathy Gap and associated

"COULD A GREATER MIRACLE TAKE PLACE THAN FOR US TO LOOK THROUGH EACH OTHER'S EYES FOR AN INSTANT?"

HENRY DAVID THOREAU

loneliness slowly spreads across our lives and entire organisations. It is hard to have the levels of energy it takes to empathise when your own mental health is suffering and as stress increases, empathy decreases further. A vicious circle, with a human deficiency at its core, begins.

Many people blame social media for much of the exclusion or alone-ness we feel, for its hooking of us into 24/7 screens that reflect fake ideals or unreal realities, but I don't think that's totally the case. Although the screen-to-screen relationships that we have today are certainly detrimental to true connection, we have always had books, tales, and fables reflecting the wondrous lives of others. Never before in history, however, were we so impacted, in such a profoundly sad way, by the stories we were accessing. Sure, the content is now always-on and closer to our daily lives, and the reach is exponential, but I don't blame the medium, I blame the usage of the medium. It's not the storytelling *medium* at fault, it's the way it's being used: Cyberbullying, cruel commentary, or unnecessary sharing are all reflections of the people posting, not the platform they are posting on. Something is brewing in society and the platforms are simply reflecting that. Social media itself is the surface, the voice, of an issue that can make people feel ever more left out, isolated, or targeted in an always-on timeline. The reality is that Millennials and Gen Z's have recognised that there is something much deeper missing from their work-life equation than what is reflected on their phone screens. As online dialogue continues to grow exponentially, we hold more of our conversations on a social platform than we do in real life, often leaving us segregated in one-sided conversation and making the medium not so social after all. It is the fact that we are alone, and not the fact that we are 'on' social media, that is fuelling the problem.

LONELINESS AS A HUMAN IDENTITY CRISIS

It is ironic then that as the world starts to actively look for deeper purpose it finds itself feeling lonelier and more isolated than ever. The collision of a social and financial tightening has created a hole that people are desperately trying to fill with as many real human connections as they can. The sad thing is that the more we search, the more acutely aware we are that perhaps these connections are no longer there to be found in our businesses.

Ever since World War I ended, and up until the 2008 crash, many people found their value defined by consumption and a never-ending swirl of promotions, pay raises, and bonuses to justify their everyday existence. It helped them hide away from any social isolation issues by filling their lives with financial replacements and rewards. Whilst the world recovered to a certain degree in the years that followed the 2008 crash, we have never truly got back on top economically, and today that leaves us with companies that don't, or are unable to, give rewards as they used to. We have lost the financial anchor that was filling the social hole. The consistency of pay rises and bonuses has significantly reduced and the workforce is having to look for new ways to measure their perceived value.[xlii] The generations in the workforce today have to define their worth and success by something much deeper than money alone, and the impact is that the purpose behind the hours they commit to work becomes ever more important.

As we explored previously, people are at their happiest when they are together. There is a reason, after all, that solitary confinement is one of the worst punishments. As Dr Craig Haney states: *"Human identity is socially created, we understand ourselves by our relationships with others"*.[xliii] By separating us from others that we identify with, we rapidly become sad and distressed. At its simplest, we find happiness and meaning by sharing in and connecting with other people's lives. When these connections disappear, we have trouble defining who we are. Loneliness is a punishment that humans, and many other animals, struggle with as a physical manifestation and not just an emotional one. Just think of the limp, dejected bodies of dogs left in shelters for a long time. They, like us, are social beings, and loneliness is a heavy and torturous emotion impacting both the mental and physical wellbeing of the animal or person. Dolphins, whales, cows, horses, goats, elephants, and deer are other animals that we know carry a similar suffering to us, and some have even been known to die of loneliness. It is not just a feeling that we hold, it is a total body experience and it can truly hurt. It is a heavy burden to carry and it has a cumulative effect on us, becoming heavier and harder to carry over time. The further apart we become the less empathy we see.

Sadly, loneliness issues are now global and are not only isolated to certain countries such as the USA or UK (where over 65 percent of people consider the television or their pet their main source of company) that are perhaps more open about the statistics.[xliv] In Canada the share of solo households is 28 percent, and across the European Union it is 34 percent.[xlvi] If people are alone physically at home, they often continue to feel alone and isolated within their working hours, and very soon loneliness is an all-day, seven days a week issue. Living on either side of this growing Empathy Gap isn't just about the actual feeling or sadness of loneliness but more about its consequences on the health and long-term wellness of populations of people. A rather scary analysis in 2015, which pooled data from seventy studies following 3.4 million people over seven years, found that lonely individuals have a 26 percent higher chance of dying prematurely, a figure that rose to 32 percent if they lived alone.[xlviii] If that isn't a screaming cry to leaders to work harder at making people feel happier by connecting to them and to each other in their working hours, then I don't know what is.

The rising desire for community living spaces, co-working environments, and dense social networking groups further proves that there is a growing social movement to address this greater need for connection and cohesion. What is interesting is the reach and breadth of how this materialises. The shared spaces and co-working environments we see in buildings all over cities are not the only ways in which people are trying to overcome the Empathy Deficit that they feel. Cornelia Geppert, creator and founder of the game Sea of Solitude by Electronic Arts, launched in July 2019, became the first artist (at the time of writing) to create a game with the earnest goal of "helping a wide-reaching number of people cope with loneliness".[xlix] This is a game actually *built* on empathy. Cornelia explains that the goal of the game is to make people *"really understand and experience the power of this emotion"* that is sweeping through so many people's lives. It is a beautiful example of empathetic influence in action on a very wide scale. The game is a superb representation of the risk and reach of the global loneliness struggle that is impacting so many people today, and Cornelia has become a leader willing to address the problem head on. After releasing the game, Cornelia was bombarded with thousands of fans who wrote to her to say that they *"felt hope for a better future"* simply by playing the game.[l] Online there was a 'sea' of people talking about the fact that the game gave them the ability to connect over their loneliness and that that was a therapy in and of itself, a shared experience connecting us with one of humanity's oldest emotions in the most modern of ways. Well done, Cornelia!

The game, which is both a social tool and a support structure, inspires me as a creative leader to think more about how to address these deeply powerful connectivity issues differently. It is not all about placing a pool table and free snacks in the staff canteen; rather it's about how and why we create an environment that actively solves some of the deeper issues. The purpose and the story of the environment, and the thinking behind it, is even more key than the facets of its physical form alone, whether that is connectivity, inclusivity, escapism, meditation, or inspiration. Understanding the needs of the team and how to address them is exactly what the team needs to grow and thrive. Satya Nadella, an avid believer in the role of empathetic influence within corporations and who has seen the value of Microsoft double its value from k302.2

billion to k681.6 billion since the time of his appointment (winning him the CEO of the Year award according to Forbes), will tell you that the secret to success in business is indeed exactly this: *"Empathy,"* he says, *"is the secret to success. The key to everything is empathy, because nothing is more effective and fruitful than the ability to walk in the shoes of others."* He continues, *"The value that I have really learned to appreciate deeply, and which I talk about a great deal is empathy. I don't think it is simply a 'nice to have' but I believe it is at the centre of the agenda for innovation here at Microsoft."*[li]

DISCONNECT TO CONNECT

Although games such as Sea of Solitude have a hugely powerful ability to connect people virtually, which can be very supportive, it doesn't solve the challenge of deep connections in the *real* world. Somewhere between the digital social revolution, our empty apartments, siloed workstation and smartphone screens, we have stopped truly connecting with those around us. We are forever connected and yet not connecting at all, and although I don't think we can 'blame' social media, which is fundamentally just a series of media *channels*, there is no doubt that our constant connection to these digital platforms is leading to an increasing desire for authentic interpersonal connections offline. As open-plan life sweeps cities and we engross ourselves in new ways of finding peace or time out, we often increase the gap without meaning to. Simply considering the headphone-clad world that we are surrounded by every day on our commute, in the office, or in the mall further deepens the understanding of the scale of this disconnection. As we disappear into our own disconnected musical environment, our aloneness, even when surrounded by hundreds of other people, is ever on the up. We cycle in headphones, we travel in headphones, we study, read, commute, and eat lunch in headphones. Maybe we should blame Bose and Beats in part for the increasing disconnection simply for making tuning out 'cool'. I jest, of course, but the more you study the social evidence the more you realise that the areas of social and popular culture fuelling the Empathy Gap are incredibly diverse and some of them are hidden in plain sight, under the guise of a new style trend or tech innovation.

A CHALLENGE OF THE YOUNG

Claudia Hammond, who instigated a survey for the BBC called the Loneliness Experiment, has a host of data suggesting that today it is the young, the Millennials, who are the loneliest. She found that only 27 percent of people over seventy-five stated they *"often feel lonely"*, whereas in the sixteen- to twenty-eight-year-old bracket, the numbers were over 40 percent.[lii] No wonder this group of people, the future of our workforce and the consumers buying our brands, are asking for a reset on how they engage with leadership and organisations. They are screaming out for change, not only because they want it, but because, for their health and wellbeing, they need it.

Of all the research I did into these traits of modern humanity and our isolation issues, the research from the World Health Organisation and the Centers for Disease Control and Prevention (CDCP) on youth suicide rates was the most chilling. According to the CDCP, the suicide rate among people aged ten to twenty-four increased 56 percent between 2007 and 2017 and suicide is now Gen Z's second leading cause of death, with this group more likely to report loneliness and despair.[liii] Unbearably sad data. What on earth have we let happen when one of the leading causes of death for our youth, our future, is ending their own lives? This epidemic is even worse in Z's than it is in Millennials, and the data suggests that Gen Z might be most at risk for mental illness.[liv]

The need to make a change is now. Always-on working hours, ever rising pressure and expectations, disconnected management (and societies), a lack of Regenerative Leadership, and autocratic structures are simply not going to lead to change that can turn around this utterly preposterous trend. We need an intervention, and as the adults, the leaders and the inspiration in the room, it's up to us to do it. To turn our hearts and open our eyes to the fact that we cannot keep running our businesses and organisations with a *growth-at-all-costs* mindset while the impact is literally killing those who are part of the journey. Whatever your shareholders or holding company is demanding of you, there have to be times when we quite simply do not, cannot, deliver year on year growth or increased output. Especially if the year before saw fantastic results. We need to look at our people beyond our profit and make a call as leaders on when to say, "*not this year*", however unpopular that makes us short term. Perhaps we should be seriously considering holding hands as global leaders, from all walks of society, to stop talking about the issues and to start looking for regenerative thinking that will create cohesive mutually beneficial environments that create a *ripple* between people's personal health and our own business success? Work-life balance may be hard to perfect, but a level of sustainable work-life *integration* should be the focus on leadership thinking in 2020 and beyond.

Luckily, governments and local bodies worldwide are beginning to recognise this gap in empathetic leadership, and they too are committing to the need to address the problem. We are now seeing a host of community programs and social connection systems popping up to try and slow the momentum. Sadly, the reality is that this trend has been gathering steam, globally, for decades and it is already responsible, in part, for the chronic physical and emotional illnesses (including burnout, corporate anxiety, high blood pressure, and a trail of business minds leaving the workforce for freelance life) plaguing working people today.[lv]

The question on everyone's minds as 2020 rolled out was whether the extended lockdown, slow down, and habitual home working caused by the COVID-19 virus would be what finally enforced long-term behavioural change? Although no one would have ever wished for such a tragedy to impact our world, the pandemic did create an opportunity for both Millennials and older leadership teams to reassess what is possible, and what is needed, for true employee wellness. Although enforced and incredibly stress-inducing in many cases, the lockdown process did create momentum for people everywhere to reassess their feelings, reconsider remote and flexible working, and begin to come to terms with the decisions they wanted to make for optimal work and life cohesion. Their experience changed and their expectations followed suit.

It is not only in the post-COVID-19 era but also at a time in current social history that we have an opportunity to help people, to support them, connect them, and build them up. In my own business turnaround story, I saw personally and directly how kindness and compassion are contagious, and at its most simple, how the more we consciously commit to these facets within organisational culture, the more our teams will, too. Habits and culture are created at the top, and it follows that a commitment to a behavioural change means that our impact is far wider reaching, touching the families, children, and even the supporting members of our teams' families or neighbours (who may not even live in the same city or country as we do).

As business leaders, we truly can change the world, and without a doubt, when we look at the state of the world today, we surely need to try.

Chapter 9

THE DEFICIT DIAGNOSIS

As we have now established, ever since 2006, the Empathy Deficit that Obama referred to has been widening as a global social issue that impacts our daily lives, and our businesses, in a profound way. Obama could clearly see it coming. During that same year he gave an impressive speech to Northwestern University graduates at a graduation ceremony. I am including a snippet of that speech here. I know very little of politics, but I do know that any leader who has the power to reach a wide audience has a responsibility to help others think and see things differently and, for me, this speech does exactly that. If you pop over to YouTube and put in "Northwestern commencement, Obama" you can watch it in full. It is of course rather larger reaching and more philosophical than my focus in this book, but it gives a great foundation to how big-picture thinkers see the problem impacting the world and people around us.

"...we live in a culture that discourages empathy. A culture that too often tells us our principal goal in life is to be rich, thin, young, famous, safe, and entertained. A culture where those in power too often encourage these selfish impulses.

They will tell you that the Americans who sleep in the streets and beg for food got there because they're all lazy or weak of spirit. That the inner-city children who are trapped in dilapidated schools can't learn and won't learn and so we should just give up on them entirely. That the innocent people being slaughtered and expelled from their homes half a world away are somebody else's problem to take care of.

I hope you don't listen to this. I hope you choose to broaden, and not contract, your ambit of concern. Not because you have an obligation to those who are less fortunate, although you do have that obligation. Not because you have a debt to all of those who helped you get to where you are, although you do have that debt. It's because you have an obligation to yourself. Because our individual salvation depends on collective salvation. And because it's only when you hitch your wagon to something larger than yourself that you will realize your true potential—and become full-grown..."

-Barack Obama, Northwestern University, 2006[lvi]

The funny thing is, even in an industry like my own, which is built on understanding people and the trends impacting society, no one is really talking about the need for empathy as a theme at scale. Obama's speech is fifteen years old and yet the practice and conversation within corporate leadership teams, to place human values before shareholder value, is still in its infancy. Again, this is not to say that leadership teams *shouldn't* be focused on creating shareholder value—of course they need to be—but simply that we must bring the emotional intelligence of empathic engagement to the table, and our teams, more often if we are to make that value sustainable in the decade of business ahead.

TEAM VOICES AS AN INSTRUMENT OF CHANGE

There is a critical need to get back to the humanity of our industries if we are to sustain the levels of output and inspiration that our businesses increasingly demand. The connections between us as humans are the glue that allows us to build on each other's ideas, to brainstorm effectively, and to feel the level of comfort required to truly co-operate for the success of a project. One of the side effects of a detached leader and their team is that the distance between them creates a powerful emotional barrier in the form of self-censorship. I suspect you have seen occasions in the workplace when the gap between senior leaders and their teams results in a gradual separation of trust and engagement between them and everyone else? It becomes all about 'us and them' versus 'you and me', and following that quickly comes a lack of honesty and self-censorship to such a level that eventually whole groups of individuals are shutting off their true potential from their role. This may be due to lack of motivation, a personal distrust, or simply a lack of engagement, but fundamentally it dissuades teams from giving their true value to the greater picture. Self-censorship can arise from two main areas of concern. First, the fear of not being heard, of being ignored or misunderstood. This creates a negative slew of ripple effects such as shame and discomfort. Second, the fear of not being accepted for the opinion shared. Both fears come from a lack in the team's social construct and not necessarily from a lack of self-confidence in the individual. Directly, it is the deficit of empathy leading to a deficit of

"IT SEEMS LIKE WE HAVE AN EMPATHY SHORTAGE, AN EMPATHY DEFICIT. WE'VE BECOME SO CYNICAL IT ALMOST SEEMS NAÏVE TO BELIEVE WE UNDERSTAND EACH OTHER."

BARACK OBAMA

communication and it's a problem that has huge financial drawbacks that can be avoided or reversed. **A leader with generosity of emotions encourages their team in such a way that they don't feel the need to self-censor.** Under open cultures, when detachment isn't an issue, teams talk, share, stand up, build on each other, and are generous with their thinking. They are fast to respond with high-energy answers that often have higher strategic potential. They show up more, take fewer days off, and engage on a more consistent basis.

As we move into a decade when our organisations require ever more creativity, innovation, and disruptive thinking to compete, the existence of self-censorship within a business will have wide-reaching detrimental effects on our ability to deliver and stay ahead. The key here is that the evolution of an uncensored, open team culture is entirely within our grasp. Given our brains are 'plastic' in their ability to mould and change depending on the stimuli and information we feed them, we are entirely able to control the amount of empathy we encourage into our team relationships. After all, as our work and personal lives become ever more intertwined, an inclusive culture where people feel able to voice their opinions and ideas is going to allow for pooling of value as well as friendship. We know the rules of the game are changing and, in

> *A leader with generosity of emotions encourages their team in such a way that they don't feel the need to self-censor.*

a time when diversity and inclusion are more important than ever, the teams that are able to openly express themselves and feel recognised for this will finish first. The reward for their input is not only a greater output but also an output with a higher perceived value. Connecting as humans before connecting as 'colleagues' is to awaken our shared humanity and experience genuine fulfilment from our working hours. It overcomes the barriers of the 'alone- ness' so deeply impacting society, and it builds bridges between sets of culturally diverse team members. Create the opportunity for people to connect, to understand each other's needs and traits, and then give them a mutual goal and we will see the best of teamwork and growth.

Although understanding each other is not often debated as an important skillset, we are failing at large to develop the need for industry-led training and communication with the same clarity and focus we develop consumer advertising campaigns. There is an immediate need to target and reach leaders worldwide to remind them and convince them of the importance of their teams' needs. We need to reach the minds, hearts, and common sense of the leading organisations worldwide and to do so with speed. I would suggest that we need to move our focus from the 'changing landscape' or 'complexities of today's ever-evolving buyer', or any of the other three hundred things we write media columns about, and instead focus on ourselves, and on our people, and on how we connect; that we focus on driving an imperative for regenerative and conscientious leadership that protects and influences people positively and sustainably and stops the decline of empathy worldwide.

On our current path, this synchronicity between teams is dangerously at risk of going missing altogether. If we allow this to happen it will be alongside our staff, the best of our output, and all of our world-changing ideas still to come.

Chapter 10

LOVE ME NOT

The truth is I don't love my job.

The actual day-to-day job? Nope.

But I do love my work.

It took me a long time to realise this, and to work out the difference, but between 2015 and 2017 I did just that. I was living and working in Singapore, alone and with plenty of time to master my own destiny.

Whether it was my natural affinity to living in tropical climates, the sweet traditional Singaporean tea that I could sip every morning, or the heavy rains that washed away the heavy days, I realised it's not my job I love. It's my work. It is the ability to impact people's lives, especially those I get to know personally, by turning up to work every day and solving problems, that drives me in my passion and my career.

From the moment I joined this industry as a twenty-three-year-old account executive, I knew exactly where I wanted to go. Getting to the top had never been about power, money, or fame but simply about the joy of what I knew I would be able to do more of, with every promotion I got. The more senior I got, the more I was able to give and to give back, albeit via things that were often in very 'ad agency' kinds of ways. It was as if only in ever-more-senior roles could I prove that empathy, kindness, and human connection were valuable concepts in the business world today. Concepts that held financial power and business impact. Not because I needed the title to do so, but because other leaders in my sphere of influence needed my title before they could listen.

Over the years there were many naysayers who disagreed with my conviction for empathy as a leadership trait to live by, and that in itself was enough to keep me working around the clock. It saw me flying from a junior executive to the Strategic Director and Board Member of a fantastically special advertising agency by the age of thirty, with an unending energy. I was a corporate ad girl if there ever was one. I never took my annual leave and I relished being the most reliable person at the table. I loved what I did and I was certain from day one that I would never change career.

It was therefore immensely surprising to me, my family, and every person I have ever worked with, when in 2016 I decided that the 'not loving' of my day job was enough to make me leave the corporate world of advertising. For a while.

I was looking for a deeper purpose and clarity around the impact I was making on the world. I wasn't running away as much as running toward a new goal and a powerful need to help the industry in a more impactful way. My strong belief in human decency and kind leadership above all else meant I was profoundly disturbed by employee engagement levels that were at an all-time low. Watching the health and emotional wellbeing of team members who were being stretched to the impossibly sharp edge of the moment when work entirely takes over life, was almost a painful experience for me. Life shouldn't be this way. How long will we let our health and emotional wellbeing slide before we all say *enough is enough?*

Having worked in healthcare marketing for a few years for GlaxoSmithKline as a Vice President with Grey Group, I found that I held an innate desire to give back the gift of health and wellness to those working 24/7 trying to solve the world's marketing problems; those career ad folk who seem to be at the bottom of the list when it comes to professionals that anyone really cares to 'look after'. I suddenly couldn't think of anything else than trying to make a change for the people in my industry. I had been watching the impact up close of the stress and strain of working in advertising agencies whilst becoming very close to the world of pharmacy and consumer health and the statistics around stress-related disease and life-enhancing choices. I felt I had to try and make an impact.

THE SHORT LIFESPAN OF LIFE-CHANGING DECISIONS

Within a few months I had set up a brand name, built a website, put over seven hundred hours of night school classes into practice, and started to teach yoga therapy and Ayurvedic health as my full-time business. Before I knew it, life as an advertising director was over, and I was an entrepreneur.

I was free, I was the healthiest I had been in a decade, and I was happy. I was energised and motivated by my industry health and wellbeing dream, and I had a host of people supporting my journey. I knew that I had the experience to build a brand, and that doing so could actively improve the health and wellbeing of my industry's most exhausted and drained stars. In our fraught world, where politicians and industry leaders debate matters vital to our health in isolation of action on the ground, I was committed to provoking action. I knew then that empathy was more important than ever, both to our teams and to ourselves in the form of self-empathy, and in looking out for our bodies and minds. As our global context and competitive environments tightened—with conflict, terror, and spiralling health issues bubbling underneath them—I recognised that we all need to at least try to move the needle toward a more sustainable state of corporate wellbeing. The world was my oyster and I was entirely in awe of my new business. For a short time.

I remember the exact moment I decided to leave behind entrepreneurial life and go back to the corporate world. I was sitting at the dining room table in my countryside home in the winelands outside Cape Town. I had a handmade South African ceramic mug steaming next to me, with mint leaves from my garden. The sky was clear African blue, I was in love, and I was a business owner. Life was good and I was passionately committed to attacking the stress endemic sweeping the globe and helping people across the corporate world get well again. I had an army of people around me willing me on.

Then the phone rang. And everything changed.

My father had had a heart attack on a British Airways plane heading from Cape Town into Heathrow. His heart and my world collapsed simultaneously, and life was never quite the same. As the machines kept his heart pumping my pulse didn't stop racing and I booked a flight to go to him as soon as I could. With the genius of twenty-first-century medical magic (seriously, magic), he was healed and strong again within four months. I, however, was not. I was changed. In the split second between hanging up from that harrowing call and taking a moment to look out at my garden, I was hit with a sharp dose of clarity and I knew instantly that I was going back to my corporate career.

A DOSE OF REALITY

When faced suddenly with potential family tragedy, I realised two things instantly. First, I would never again put myself in a position where money would be a barrier between me and my loved ones (as an entrepreneur, the price of a last-minute long-haul flight had been a serious thought) regardless of how much I believed in the dream. Dreams and goals would have to be reconsidered at a later date when they could be balanced with the security I needed for my family. Second, I realised that surrounding myself with people is absolutely integral to my own happiness. I don't know why that phone call per se made me realise that, but I realised working alone was absolutely not on the top of my 'things that motivate me' list. I recognised that being able to connect daily with others was utterly key to my own wellbeing and, beyond that, I began to understand this wasn't unique to me but a deep-rooted reality for human beings. There are many benefits of working for yourself. No line management slowing things down, no formal hours, no office politics or the potential for 'toxic' environments, no desperately sad gap in empathy driving morale down and resignations up. But what people don't tell you is the other side. The fact that you no longer have anyone around you to invest in, or return the favour. There is no one to brainstorm with, no team to inspire, no one to travel the ups and downs of client life with, no one to teach you anything, share anything, or stop you in the corridor to say well done. No one asks you for advice or shares a cup of tea with you and you don't get to spend your days helping others solve problems and thrive in their days. It. Is. Lonely. And here we are again. That isolation issue that seems to be following Millennials around!

I left corporate work because I could see the impact of the Empathy Deficit on our people and I was hooked on trying to find a solve for it. For many others it is the deficit itself that drives them out. Whether you stay at work or work from home, you can't seem to avoid the isolating impact of the deficit itself. Whether you are 'alone' on a floor full of

"ATTENTION IS THE RAREST AND PUREST FORM OF GENEROSITY."

SIMONE WEIL, FRENCH PHILOSOPHER

people in an office, or spending days working from co-sharing spaces or cafés, the reality is that you need much deeper levels of connection and connectivity than any shared environment can offer. In the months that followed my father's heart attack I realised that I needed a team around me if I was to find my own strength in continuing to deliver empathy, and I needed to be back in the corporate world to do so.

DISCOVERING THE EMPATHY DEFICIT FOR MYSELF

During this time, I began to study connectedness, human behaviour, and social norms in corporate environments. I was fascinated by the psychology behind why I was feeling the way I was about having a team around me, and why it was that my connection to my teams fulfilled me and drove me like it did. It wasn't long until I understood that empathy and empathetic connection were entirely at the core of everything that motivated me personally and drove me to do my best throughout my career to date. It was a couple of years later, in 2018, that I dug deeper into this and began to write this book, but in those months in the South African winelands, as I cooked by candlelight when the power cut for hours at a time, I realised that there was absolutely a missing link, and it wasn't only the lack of light in my home: it was the lack of connectedness that impacts entrepreneurs all around the world and that no one talks about.

As I connected with other entrepreneurs in far-flung corners of the planet, I discovered that it certainly wasn't only me who missed the corporate world and the people who inhabit it. It's not so 'cool' to admit these things as a budding entrepreneur, but under the secrecy and anonymity of social media I found plenty of others out there who missed the connectivity of working in teams and groups and were struggling because of it. There were lots of negatives they didn't miss about the office, but they would also admit that perhaps they had run a little faster than they needed to out of an office environment, and they were now feeling alone and cut off. They missed it. We all want to be understood and connected to others around us; it drives us and motivates us and it does so from almost the moment we are born. Working alone, out of sight and out of earshot of other people, cuts us off from things we need in order to thrive: to be seen and to be heard and to put into practice what is perhaps our quintessential human instinct— to share in the understanding of someone else's reality. This instinct is with us from the moment a baby enters the world. The moment the infant arrives screaming onto the planet they have the ability to connect with their mother, through eye contact and touch. It's natural and it not only creates a sense of safety and connection, it also justifies and confirms their existence. *"Hi Mum. I. Am. Here. See me. Listen to me."* Or as the Zulus would say:

"I see you."

"I am here."

Biologically, we have been built to form a connection and understanding with our fellow humans as a core part of our nature. As a baby grows they frequently watch their parents and siblings for signs as to how they are feeling and what works to drive deeper connectivity between them. From a very young age they seem to show empathy for others. Infants have been seen to cry when babies around them cry, and young toddlers can recognise pain or upset in their parents' faces well before they can talk to them about it. Before full conversation is an option, the eye contact and facial expressions between the parents, siblings, and babies continually reinstate our understanding of each other's moods, desires, or suffering.

There is a reason that parenting books worldwide advise parents to kneel down, at eye level, when explaining 'bad' behaviour to babies and young children. The need to connect through your eyes, your facial expression, and your body language in a way that makes the child feel 'seen' and understood is infinitely more effective than when the adult distances themselves from a standing height. The connection at eye level creates an empathetic understanding that ultimately allows for feedback to be more openly and effectively received and understood. As a mum of a toddler, I can vouch for this as true, and from a leadership POV (although I don't need to kneel to give feedback to my teams!) I can absolutely commit to the fact that leaning in and making eye contact makes even the toughest of discussions both easier and more clearly and successfully received. If you are working alone as an entrepreneur or a freelancer, who is there to create this confirmation of your professional existence, success, or craft? It is often a painfully lonely reality.

I am not saying no one should ever leave the corporate world, far from it. But I am saying that as this becomes a new normal, full-of-benefits lifestyle, we now have two sides of a leadership coin to address. First, the side that drives us to conscientiously support and nurture our teams' talent so that they might decide not to join the escape train and leave the corporate world, and second, our commitment to those outside of our office-bound reach, due to their decision to work alone, by extending our empathetic energy and focus to them, too, every time we or our teams engage with them. Making these small businesses or independent teams feel valued as extended team members of larger corporate organisations is such a simple yet critical skill to imbue into our organisations. It will have far-reaching impact if we can truly get it right. If empathy is the human language of mutual gain, it follows that for many entrepreneurs or solo workers, this lack of humanity's language on a frequent basis is an issue that impacts them deeply. The companies that overcome this empathy gap with their external teams and freelance partners will not only gain from far more return and productivity, but those external partners will gain far more from the partnership than a pay slip alone.

CORPORATE HAPPY GLUE

It is not acceptable that our corporate environment is making people, by the bus load, choose to leave their industry to find something that better resembles a healthy life.[lviii] I promised myself from the moment that I decided to return to work to address this in the next role I stepped into. I wanted to find an organisation that would allow me to draw on the training in human values, wellness, and evolutionary health that I had completed. I was determined to prove that these values had their place in the corporate world, too, and not just in entrepreneurial life. I wanted to create a 'glue' at scale that not only connected me to the organisation but that would also inspire and motivate the teams around me to stay and thrive alongside me. This time, I decided I would find a way to influence the leadership lens and touch the emotional wellness of the industry around me, without sacrificing my family balance with the chaos and insecurity of setting up alone. And so, my journey back to an office and to a team began.

BACK TO MY FUTURE

Once I set my mind on re-joining the corporate world, everything happened quickly. I found myself a phenomenal opportunity in Dubai running one of the fastest-growing global agency brands for the Middle East and Africa. It was with huge anticipation and energy that I packed up my life and moved to the desert. At the time I saw it as a chance to take on a growth project for a small agency and put my beliefs around empathetic and Regenerative Leadership back into action, to truly pressure test them. I was passionately committed to putting the health and wellness of my new team at the top of the agenda and building an organisational test case that happy, centred, fulfilled teams provoke growth and business success, with both stability and sustainability at the core. I boarded an Emirates flight north with four suitcases and a baby in tow, blissfully unaware of what I was flying into. As we touched down in Dubai for the first time, my eyes were about to be opened wide.

It was reality, and not the local scorpions, that bit the hardest when I finally got into my new role.

What I was confronted with on arrival at my new company was a reality that looked far from anything I had been told about when I decided to move my entire life to a new continent. In fact, the picture and the reality were not only disconnected, they weren't even from the same hemisphere. As the first weeks unfolded it was an understatement to say I was angry and entirely overwhelmed, and that in the short term I lost my leadership compass altogether. This was a business that was so far from being empathetically driven, or even prepared for empathy, and there was barely a shadow of the foundation I had bought into.

WARNING: TROUBLING TIMES AHEAD

I remember vividly the first sign of trouble. It was day two and the then leader had organised a team drinks for my welcome. Anyone who has ever been to a team drinks event knows exactly what it's like: smiling people, entertaining banter, bountiful conversation, team storytelling, general energy and connectivity. Anyone who has ever been to a team drinks in an *advertising agency* can escalate the energy of such an occasion up a notch or three. They are generally happy events that encapsulate the best of relaxed, happy humans who want to pass time together as a team in a social setting.

But not this team.

Not this advertising agency.

As we arrived in the hotel bar that evening, the team awkwardly settled around a table in uncomfortable silence, eyes darting expectantly from the old boss to me, the new one. People looked anywhere but at each other, and the silence was deafening. I held back the urge to laugh into the awkwardness. The atmosphere was icy. As I tried to navigate some level of personal connection with this new group of people, I soon realised this was going to be very, very hard work. Not only wasn't there any banter, there was barely any oxygen!

No one leant in, no one chatted. The team glanced between their watch and studying the menu, all the while trying to be polite to the 'new girl'. I sat there, part fascinated, part concerned, and part entirely confused, with a weird feeling somewhere between wanting to run home to my baby and staying and grabbing hold of their hands and asking them all individually what was wrong. I knew in time I could do both, but for now I had to spectate and start uncovering the edges that were now all mine to soften and rebuild.

We poured one drink each and we left, every person as relieved as the next that the event was over. By the time I got into my taxi the concern had left an aggravating tug that something was seriously wrong, and potentially much more wrong than the end of the second day could possibly have yet revealed. I crept home to my temporary apartment and looked down in the darkness at my sleeping daughter, holding tightly to the edge of her crib and asking myself what on earth had I taken on here.

I kept reminding myself that I had wanted a challenge! Although I had no idea how I was going to fix it, by morning three I knew with great clarity why I had been brought in. This group of people needed much more than a new structure to work within; they needed a whole new start. My desire to start building empathetic evidence in the corporate world had clearly begun. If I was ever going to prove the power of empathetic influence and Regenerative Leadership to turn around a business, the slate had been handed to me. Fate had intervened and I had everything I needed to create the proof I so wanted to deliver.

BE CAREFUL WHAT YOU WISH FOR

Did your mother ever tell you to "*be careful what you wish for?*" Mine certainly did, and as with most mums most of the time, she was of course right.

My handover period was tumultuous and overwhelming. I watched teams sit deliberately in silence in meetings, eyes to the floor, and uncomfortably make their way through compulsory 'team breakfast' events. Days passed as people entered and left meetings silently, awkwardly staring down at steaming cups of chai tea and passing the hours as they wished away the shared time. It wasn't that the people disliked each other—I could see genuine warmth in the glances between them—but simply that they were working in a business where they had to be given *permission* to talk, to leave at the end of the day, and to be who they are. Their work was far from their own and it was fear and not friendship that connected them. Their confidence had been shattered in an environment where they could be openly criticised for anything from their working ability, to their dress sense, to their hairstyle, to their accent. There were a couple of young members of that team who were so debilitated by their experience that they had become unable to even speak. It was devastatingly sad.

This feels unimaginable in Western companies due to the legalities of employee care, but in some emerging markets there are cultural differences that make this entirely feasible. For these youngsters, when their sentences did come out it was in barely audible sets of words pulled together amongst deep stutters, low confidence, and skittish eyes. It was a painful corporate reality. I knew change would take time, but I also knew I didn't have much of that time to build belief and regenerate this team before they all checked out entirely. Time was of the essence.

I learnt about the 'secrets' of an Empathy Gap during that time. I learnt that often these 'secrets' within corporations and their people are unsaid and unseen so that those at exec level are altogether unaware of them. I discovered that there are secrets that people carry into their personal lives, secrets of unhappiness, esteem issues, loneliness, and disregard. Secrets that take away the value of a team's shared humanity. Secrets that reside within walls and go unnoticed until someone new arrives and questions the status quo.

It was utterly amazing to me that this 'attack' on people had been carrying on under a cloak of secrecy. It made me quickly realise how much damage can be done within the small and direct circle of one leader. I think we underestimate how powerful our leadership style and our decision to invest, or not, in our people is, and how far that choice ripples into people's homes and family lives. At the time, no one at the top knew what was going on in the company I had joined, and that created a deep sense of responsibility in me, not just for the shrouded realities that I was uncovering but for the reversal of them at a pace. I spent many evenings wondering how much more corporate bullying and turmoil was happening under wraps out there in larger organisations and I grew increasingly confident that the secrets hidden within strangled teams needed sharing on a far wider level than my corporate world alone. At the time I had enough on my hands focusing inward before looking further afar, but it was the beginning of a powerful reality for me that did eventually result in me jumping on a plane to Singapore and writing this book.

SHOOTS OF REGROWTH

One of my first acts in the early days was to cancel all the dreadful forced social occasions (with the encouragement of an extremely relieved team) and hence commenced nine months of healing before the team ever socialised together again. The next time they did get together, it was by their own free will and it was a joyous affair.

It may seem odd to develop a summary of an organisation's health by their social habits (bearing in mind that in the Middle East many people don't drink alcohol so it wasn't a drinking culture but a social cohesion issue), but in the advertising industry particularly, a team without camaraderie is like a creative without a MacBook: lost, out of place, and unable to live to its potential. Social cohesion underpins so much of success, given relationships are the fuel of nearly all progress. It is an outdated leader that still believes it is power that leads to growth. It is the strength of your relationships that drives the strength of your corporate resilience and competitive edge, and it will be people, time and again, that lead to organisational resolution and regeneration. It is well- known that people produce their best work when they are connected, sharing stories and life experiences and generally in sync with their colleagues. Happy people do better work. Self-censorship is to creativity what kryptonite is to Superman. Utterly debilitating.

My first steps to rebuilding the social cohesion, by creating some short-term space between people, were the first shoots of our 'Spring' season; the beginning of regrowth as individuals and as a team on its way to a new level of flourishing. I knew then as I do now that creativity thrives in environments when the human spirit, and therefore the mind, is at its happiest, and this was at its most basic my goal of those initial months. I began telling everyone I met, internally and externally, that our only goal was to become the *Happiest Agency in the Middle East.* Given the neuroplasticity of the brain (the brain's ability to flex and mould to new information) words are extremely powerful, and these words were critical. Not only did they name my intention in the simplest and most motivating form, but they also explicitly communicated that we would be putting people first, no matter what. They became critical words and people started to share them outwardly. It wasn't long until they became a key catch phrase for uniting our team and our clients with a brand-new agency to come.

As that first summer unrolled it felt like every day brought a new problem of unbelievable proportions, and they were all mine to fix. We were fired twice by large clients in my first four weeks, and half the office admitted they either had or were about to resign. Needless to say, it was bleak. My second decision in that time was to take down all the walls, get rid of the office I had been given, and to sit with the team. If they were going to face the turmoil of a total turnaround and relaunch, we were going to do it together. Whatever side of the coin people fell on—those who loved the change or those who hated it—we were going to confront it as one. I knew there would be fallout, but I also knew that the only way to ensure a soft landing was to be as deeply connected to the day to day as possible. Love me or hate me for what was to come, no one would be able to doubt a sound strategy, my commitment to bringing it to life gently, or the fact that we were doing so as one team.

THE WEIGHT OF CHANGE

I have to be honest, there were many days when I doubted that any level of Regenerative Leadership could save the sinking ship. I was wrong, of course, but it was daunting; some days the ethical and human issues were almost too much to handle. I turned up day after day and put on a brave face and a wide smile with as much passion as I could muster, but it was a joyless task in those months, a marathon that no one had put me in training for, and it felt like an impossible task. It was in those moments that I realised there was going to be only one way to take this team out of the quicksand that we were clearly in, and that was by using the only thing I knew could possibly work when every chip was down: **empathy**.

In the August of that summer I closed the agency for a week. We had a long weekend and I extended it to allow a solid week-long break for all of us. It had never been done before, and at that stage I didn't know it would be the first in a long line of 'firsts', but it was instinctive and necessary. I didn't know what else to do but create some space in the chaos. I knew that upon return from that break, the changes I had in mind had to move from ideas to action, fast.

I have clear memories of sitting alone for the five days, in a local golf club, watching the city skyline from across a driving range as I mapped out an eighteen-month plan that I hoped would turn the dial from zero to somewhere near hero in the months ahead. With every soya latte that appeared on my table, the waiters became friendlier and the local golfers began welcoming me to breakfast each morning. Those gentlemen, whose names I never knew, became critical characters in my rebuild story. Their kindness and jovial banter reignited my soul a little more in every day that passed and they welcomed me to a city I was trying to call 'home'. Their empathy for me, a woman alone, clearly trying to overcome a challenging time and strangely a non-golfer in a golfer's world, had an unprecedented impact on my strength and confidence. I finally felt able to remind myself I had been chosen for this role and that the fifteen years behind me may not necessarily have taught me these skills exactly, but they had offered me everything I needed to face this challenge.

On the final morning of that week I had an acute memory of the days back at the dining room table in South Africa. The energy I had, the bright blue sky, and the feeling that anything was possible when you put the health and wellbeing of an industry before all else. My yogic studies and my learnings from GlaxoSmithKline came flying back simultaneously and it became clearer than ever that the answer was really quite simple: **put people above all else and everything else will follow**.

The Empathy Advantage was born.

The Empathy Advantage: Put people above all else and everything else will follow.

Note: The issues I was unfolding were and are misaligned to the culture and values of the wider global brand and no one in the company at that time, or since, was complicit in the actions in the local market. I am grateful to the chairman for supporting my instinct and encouraging my empathy approach to our business strategy.

"INFINITE GROWTH OF MATERIAL CONSUMPTION IN A FINITE WORLD IS AN IMPOSSIBILITY."

E. E. SCHUMACHER,
STATISTICIAN AND ECONOMIST

Chapter 11

FIGHTING AND FLIGHTING CORPORATE HEALTH

I returned to the office and the weight I felt I had been carrying had gone. I felt I could stand taller, smile from the heart, and truly begin a journey. The team felt better, too, and the energy was palpable.

Coffee by coffee, meeting by meeting, one person at a time, I used instinct and gut feel to work out what hurt the most and how we could fix it. Actively listening, leaning in, sharing the realities of every team member or client I met, I started to work with each person personally to map out a new way for tomorrow. I spent my days unpacking hundreds of unique personal issues and step by step defining where the blocks were and how we could start to unblock them. I committed to meet with every single person personally and repeatedly. I knew the solves were going to be in deploying an ongoing wave of always-on emotional intelligence and care, on a one- to-one level with the team and the clients. Whilst analysis of the financial and new business intelligence would be of use much later down the line, in those initial months it was about debris and human diligence, not spreadsheets. My empathy was my data. Empathy was my input and it was my judgement. It was empathy that was infusing every part of my decision making. Although this process came naturally to me, it was also utterly exhausting. The results, though, were almost immediate, and as the relationships began to build in depth that was enough fuel to rocket propel my energy.

In those deeply regenerating weeks, I told myself over and over that **with time and with care would come growth**. I had to remain staunchly confident about those foundational pillars to the Empathy Advantage. The toughest part, however, was that given both the regional and the global leadership team had been kept in the dark and knew nothing of what was had been going on, I was not only digging a company out from the ashes but I was also handling the shock of extremely senior stakeholders across the world. I felt very alone in those months, and the loneliness certainly impacted my own emotional wellbeing. I learnt quickly that the deeper I connected on a personal level with my team and clients, the better we all felt so I continued to propagate this thinking as widely as I could. Connecting not only supported my own levels of anxiety (as a single mother in a broken business on a continent all alone) but also fuelled the trust and transparency with which those around me approached me and our business challenges. It united us.

I learnt that vulnerability is truly powerful. As I shared my own plight, people moved in to lighten the load. I was able to activate higher levels of empathy by opening up about my own challenges and realities. The more human I was with people, the more human they were with me. The more I shared and connected, the more people shared and connected back. Our natural herd mentality kicked in. Empathy was paving the way over a very bumpy road and making it far easier to travel together.

AN INDUSTRY-WIDE GAP

For many years people have asked me why I continue this love affair with the ad industry, despite the hours, the reduced margins, the high pressure and never-ending washing machine of dramas that surround creative output. My answer was always and remains to be *"the people and the creativity."* I have worked client side and I have worked within many of my clients' organisations, and however many I enter, I am simply hooked on the magic that advertising agencies breed. Sure, it comes with turmoil and twenty- three edits on a simple logo, but it's my 'home' and my heartland. You step into an agency, Coldplay rings out in the background, and some guy with a ponytail, jeans, and a faded beer

"IF THERE IS ANY ONE SECRET OF SUCCESS, IT LIES IN THE ABILITY TO GET THE OTHER PERSON'S POINT OF VIEW AND SEE THINGS FROM HIS ANGLE AS WELL AS YOUR OWN."

HENRY FORD

t-shirt walks past with steaming coffee, a vape, and a smile, and I simply couldn't work anywhere else.

The fact that our people are leaving at a rate of knots—the account management teams to client side (where they hope to find the holy grail of shorter hours and perceived higher control) and the creatives to freelance and home-based project work (where they hope they can escape the shorter timelines and discover shorter days)—makes me want to cry, but it also makes me want to stay. To build and regenerate, and to prove to people that this industry doesn't have to be as hard edged toward the humans who love it so. It is important that a host of us do stay, because if we all leave for similar pastures, to consult or to become a client, who will be left to love this industry into its next heyday?!

When I came back to the industry that summer, I was shocked by quite how many people were leaving and at what pace, but as I interviewed people at length in the months that followed, I was no longer remotely surprised by the industry's leaky bucket. For sure, I was in a unique situation, and there couldn't have been many agencies with issues to the extent we had, but even so, the industry was so full of detached leaders that attracting and keeping talent was becoming extremely difficult. A senior copywriter once told me that in her previous two advertising agencies she estimated 80 percent of her work never even left the building. How's that for demotivating a creative mind? Agencies seemed to only ever say no to their own people's requests, and not to their clients (however impossible they were) and the passion from their teams was, quite fairly, dwindling fast.

Over on the client side the issues were, and are, not much better. The marketers are in a constant circle of fear fused with endless admin, trying to plan campaign by metrics instead of insight, and spending more time managing stakeholders than their own campaigns. I found myself wondering daily in those months, with fresh eyes, how we allowed the marketing world, client and agency side, to become so full of fear, so corporate, and so incredibly sharp edged. I was interviewing and networking weekly, and with every additional cup of tea I became increasingly convinced that the gap between wanting to love your job and actually loving it was less a gap than a deep ravine. Of course, the

"WE HAVE BECOME SO HYPER FOCUSED ON THAT END RESULT, AND WHEN THE END RESULT IS A WIN, THE HUMAN COMPONENT OF HOW WE GOT THERE OFTEN GETS SWEPT UNDER THE PROVERBIAL RUG, AND SO DOES THE DAMAGE. WE HAVE A CRISIS IN THE WIN-AT-ALL-COST CULTURES THAT WE HAVE CREATED."

VALORIE KONDOS FIELD, RECENTLY RETIRED HEAD COACH OF THE UCLA WOMEN'S GYMNASTICS TEAM

reality was that this situation had not happened during the short time I had been out of corporate life, but the time I had taken out enabled me to see this anew. I had new eyes and new perspective, but I also had a sad heart and very heavy shoulders.

WHAT IS MACRO IS MICRO

From a big picture, macro, point of view, the complex and tumultuous state of society at large has had a huge impact on our ability to think creatively within the corporate world. The fusion of terror, unfair behaviour, bullying, and sadness in mainstream media has allowed this chaos to infiltrate our creative spirit, without us even realising. We have become desensitised to how crazy the realities we are working within are. At what point did 'another' mass mall shooting become just 'another' incident? At what point did we normalise teaching children to hide in bathroom cubicles from gunmen? And do we have any idea what the impact of this normalisation will have on the coming generations that grow up with such realities?

It is a social phenomenon we have not yet seen come to fruition when these extreme empathy gaps, resulting in bullying, violence, or antisocial behaviour, change the outlook and expectations of an entire generation. Are we going to stop and consider what this really means for our work-life reality? The fact that 85 percent of people are unhappy for five-sevenths of their week cannot be good for anyone's mental or emotional health, let alone the health of a business or society.[lix]

I soon saw that the industry was so plagued by disconnected teams, autocratic leaders, high pressure, and the realities of living in a perpetual state of stress that no one could see the wood for the trees. Leaders and teams alike didn't have the time or the mental capacity to worry about anyone else or spend any time connecting beyond the basics. The pressure on the bottom line and the focus on winning at all costs, plus shrinking timelines and lack of loyalty from clients and staff alike, meant we were in a stress-induced humanity coma.

As I researched the impact of deep stress on human behaviour, I uncovered a whole new set of retreat centres and repositioned spas in Europe and Asia that had developed a new business model pulling in clients for 'burnout' therapies and recovery. There are new industries actually opening to help us maintain and improve our health and wellness, because of the stress and strain we choose to put ourselves under in the name of business growth, career progress, or efficiency. Money is being made from a lack of focus on our humanity.

A turning point for me was when I realised that it wasn't just people's health, mental and physical, that I could see being impacted, but actually their natural ability to empathise at all. As I looked at the faces and body language of the team I inherited, and of the clients we had alienated, I could see that it was way beyond a rational choice not to connect with each other. The fact was that the team members had been under such intense stress, exhaustion, and unhappiness for so long that their ability to activate empathy and use their limbic system (the part of the brain responsible for emotions, memory, and learning) to empathise with others had dissolved over time until it was inactive. Stress and unhappiness were inhibiting their ability to empathise because the brain was prioritising the 'high risk' emotions over the need to connect with others. High stress is empathy's greatest enemy and when we are within its grasp, empathising or any form of human connection is physically an impossibility.

FIGHTING AND FLIGHTING

You have probably heard of the 'fight or flight' response. What this literally translates to is the body's response to the release of fear hormones into the bloodstream in the presence of a perceived danger. Evolution has primed our bodies to respond to threat or strain by producing hormones (the most well-known being cortisol, noradrenalin, and adrenalin) that activate key areas of our bodies to allow us to escape and escape fast, or stay and fight it out to the best of our physical ability. [lxi] Pretty much it means you pump blood to your arms, legs, and lungs in preparation to flee or attack, and your entire body is on high alert.

> *It is our role as conscientious leaders to do our absolute utmost to not play any additional role in the chronic stress that is spiraling out of control across the world.*

The impact of this response means that the body has very little energy being directed to the emotionally led parts of the brain, because everything is pumping into your muscles. When your working life (or lifestyle) is under such pressure that your body constantly feels under threat, by definition you are constantly mobilising resources away from critical parts of your body such as your gut, your elimination system, your immune system, and your higher brain systems, and sending that energy to the areas your body thinks it needs to manage a life-threatening attack. The consequences of this reach well beyond the workplace and into all areas of our lives, leaving us with impaired immune systems, poor memory, reduced focus and concentration, slowed digestion, and incomplete elimination of toxins. We take more sick days, we sleep less well, we perform at lower rates. We are less productive, less focused, and less strategic. Fundamentally, when we are under stress, we are less able and less well in all areas of our lives.

"EMPATHY IS THE MOST RADICAL HUMAN EMOTION"

GLORIA STEINEM,
JOURNALIST AND SOCIAL POLITICAL ACTIVIST

It is no wonder then that the healthcare system today is under such huge pressure from stress-related illnesses. If you can believe it, some doctors now claim that up to 90 percent of illnesses reported to GPs are stress related.[lxiii] Our bodies are chronically compromised because of the stress hormones inhibiting the immune system day in and day out. As leaders, we often enable this stress monster's grasp on our people.

I am no expert in medicine or surgery, but I do know that when an organ is transplanted, the medical team often injects the body with a form of stress hormone drug (corticosteroids) prior to implanting the new organ, disarming the immune system so that the body is less likely to reject the new organ.[lxiv] It has been proven that stress- related hormones stop our body functioning optimally and reduce the strength we have to best approach emotional challenges and relationships. It is our role as conscientious leaders to do our absolute utmost to not add to the chronic stress that is spiralling out of control. We are here to create positive ripples, not aid the negative ones.

SHORTCOMINGS TO HIGH PERFORMANCE

The inbuilt intelligence of the body and its ability to heal and face off disease is mind blowing, but we have to also remember that the physical response to threat was developed as a short-term defence system. It was not meant to last for the extended periods of time that we endure today under the perpetual stress of corporate life. This constant stress means that our own defence system, designed to protect us, is causing us harm. This fear response was, after all, based on the possibility of a sabre-toothed tiger appearing nearby, and not the long-term strain of deadlines, margin pressure, reduced budgets, and detached bosses who shout more than they share.

Today, our bodies have no idea how to distinguish between high corporate stress and a tiger or approaching army, and therefore it continually produces cortisol and adrenalin, and therein lies the problem.

For my team in those first months, and, I am sure, many others out there today, the stress-induced, high-hormone pain and panic was rampant. It makes changemaking, creative performance, or innovative thinking nowhere near anyone's core agenda. When our brains and our immunity have been starved of attention, fear is high and appetite for risk or change is nonexistent. Enduring the day to day is as much as people want to handle (even if they know that change could be for the good) and they tend to be untrusting and detached from confronting the challenges that a team needs to face as a unit. Corporate survival of the fittest is firmly in action. Under this level of discomfort, the natural response of any team will be to protect themselves from further harm, and they won't be open to adapting to a state that cares about others with any high level of commitment or energy. In a stressed state, people will only be focused on the survival of the one person they are loyal to: themselves.

It becomes obvious why this extended stress is not only hugely detrimental to people but to business performance and output as a whole. Fundamentally, the higher the disconnect and the stress, the lower the effectiveness and performance, and therefore the lower the profit, per capita. People simply cannot perform at their best under these circumstances. It's not a choice, it's evolutionary biology.

A FIGHTING JOURNEY BACK TO HEALTH

The impact of any long-term stress-led culture, like the one my team had been working within, will always be served well by an empathetic and conscious connection, but activating this takes immense practice, time, and an enduring commitment. The goal for any leader in this situation will be to take their team on a journey to **focusing back on their souls before their roles**. To find out what motivates them, grounds them, and fulfils them. To understand their purposes, their drivers, and their dislikes. To connect with them as people.

I had seen this commitment create powerful change in all walks of life, where politicians have managed empathy in an awkward environment to connect with their communities, where doctors connected with their patients more deeply through to recovery, where teachers managed to create progress amongst their most unruly students. The ability to connect empathetically has become a 'secret' key in recent times, regardless of the fact that it is actually hardwired into human nature. **When these empathetic facets are ignored or out of balance within the corporation or leadership team, stress will be like a slow-burning flame that gradually burns away the team's ability and capacity to emotionally connect at all.** More than once in the last two quarters of 2018 I questioned whether people can actually run out of empathy. Could people be pushed to their limits in such a way over time that their natural instinct to empathise was driven too deep for them to find? My research had proven the answer to be a categorical no, but I was constantly looking for reassurance in modern times that this was still the case.

In March 2019, Jacinda Ardern appeared on social media all around the world, wearing a hijab for the first time, in support of the victims of the horrific mosque attack in New Zealand.[lxvii] Although I wish this event had never occurred, her response was a sign to me that indeed the power of empathy was alive and well, and that I need not have ever doubted its power. Human beings will never lose their empathy, however deeply hidden it may be short term, but finding the right path to leveraging it was going to take significant investment of time and patience. My business turnaround would take the slow road and I gave myself eighteen months to see the Empathy Advantage deliver its results.

Chapter 12

HARNESSING THE EMPATHY ADVANTAGE

When confronted with the total corporate chaos I found in my new job, there were three truths that I clung to:

1. As humans, we **choose** to empathise. It is beneficial to us.
2. Creativity can solve anything (almost!).
3. A cup of tea can change 100 perspectives! (That's probably the Brit in me, but it does tend to be true.)

I will save discussions on creativity and tea for my podcast, but people choosing to empathise is what I want to unpack. Economists and evolutionary psychologists have struggled for many years to explain why people act in altruistic or kind ways. They are looking for the answer to why we give to charity, choose to help complete strangers, or go out of our way to donate to causes far beyond our own daily lives. After two years of researching empathy, I now know that people choose to empathise and that the empathy itself is what drives our actions. There will be science both for and against this argument, but as I embarked on the Empathy Advantage to turn around my own business, I chose to trust that I was right.

MOVING SINKING TEAMS TO IN-SYNC TEAMS

Each morning I set out to convince everyone around me that the Empathy Advantage would work and that given some time and conviction it would lead to business change. My conviction was not always met with open arms, and I was often reminded that this wasn't the most traditional of approaches. In any organisation, the intangible and slow impact of an emotional intelligence-led business turnaround strategy is not far from excruciating to many.

I spent a lot of time during those months looking to other leaders or writers for inspiration and validation of my own Empathy Advantage strategy. Sir Ken Robinson was one of them. As one of the world's leading thinkers on education, his understanding and professional opinion surrounding our ability to learn was of unending inspiration to me. I was a single mum to a toddler at the time, and every morning when she woke me up at 5 a.m. I spent time watching her and realising there was much I could learn from being her mum and applying that to my work in positive ways. Amongst many of these lessons, I learnt that when children make kind gestures or behave well, they get infinitely more value and incentive from human praise and recognition than they do from physical rewards. There are no sweets or toys in the world that make them feel as proud and as content as their parents' praise, attention, and appreciation. **I became aware at the simplest level that feeling noticed and giving our time or actions as a 'gift' to others is fundamentally rewarding and joyful for us**. The Dalai Lama said: *"If you want others to be happy, practise compassion. If you want to be happy, practise compassion."* It is such a powerfully human statement. These insights were the beginning of my journey to look to the education sector for intel for the corporate world. So long have these industries been separated yet there is so much value that could be transferred. The lessons of children and their learning capacity is of infinite value to the adults that occupy our workplaces, and so much of what we once knew as children we have long lost. As far as I see it, this is a huge opportunity to look to our youth more often. It takes a keen eye and a commitment to do so, but no practice, no mastery.

Supporting this very 'real life' insight track, brain imaging research studies have revealed that, similar to the pain indicators Dr Singer studied, the pleasure centres in the brain are just as active when we are giving something to someone else (e.g. gift/charity/support) as when we receive it ourselves. We mirror the reward as the giver and the receiver. Who knew that the entire concept behind the 'joy of giving' is actually a physical response? We really do gain enjoyment from giving, from sharing, and from looking out for others.

This was quite a pinnacle moment for me as my studies took form and I realised that being empathetic is actually joyful beyond being powerful. It makes sense, in hindsight, that humans have evolved to be both physically and emotionally rewarded for looking out for each other and to deeply enjoy connecting with those around us. Until that point I simply hadn't considered that empathy was self-serving as well as socially serving, but I relished the fact that it gave me all the more material to work with, with my team.

THE FIRST SIGNS OF REGENERATION

My Empathy Advantage strategy continued, and to my joy the results started to show. The first signs were that we won two new, small, clients, whom we took on more for the elevation of morale than the money. I wanted my people to see that we were 'wanted'. This is the greatest gift you can give to a team that has lost its mojo; reminding them: "you are seen."

At the time, some of my senior colleagues were unsure about my methods (or madness?) because our clients were costing us more than they were earning us, but I promised them that it would pay off. We needed to bring new energy into the agency and to prove that as a group we could 'win', but more importantly, we needed to give the team a *reason* to *rebuild* as a unit. I had to give them projects that they could conquer together and to give them a reason to connect. To give them the chance to empathise. Win or lose, they were able to start rebuilding a relationship and a level of empathetic understanding with each other. We needed to be 'doing' business, and in the act of business being done, slowly we were able to see change.

The only thing I purposefully deprioritised month on month were the numbers. I knew we needed to make (much) more money, as quickly as possible, but I was entirely committed to the opinion that there was just no point looking at the numbers repeatedly. They looked bad, and they were bad, but looking at them over and again meant I had to keep reliving the reality that we had too many people for too little revenue. I constantly repeated, *"Let's just give it one more month!"* but I knew this strategy wasn't a quick-fire one because the change was a human one, and human change always takes time.

Underpinning the change, I carried the constant strain of knowing that I had to eventually make changes and cuts to the team. We couldn't justify the headcount and in order to align our brand with global benchmarks, we needed a specific set of specialists. I also knew the most decent and fair way to make these cuts was to secure our base first and ensure we could make the decisions with as much strategic intent and emotional agility as possible. I set about training everyone,

"WE HAVE EVOLVED THIS POWERFUL SENSE OF IMAGINATION, THE ABILITY TO BRING TO MIND THINGS THAT AREN'T HERE. FROM THIS FOLLOW ALL KINDS OF POWERS LIKE CREATIVITY—AND UNIQUELY AND DISTINCTLY—THE POWER OF EMPATHY."

SIR KEN ROBINSON

no matter their level, on the empathetic levers we were going to grow by. Whether it was with regard to our existing clients, potential new clients, or new partners, every member of the team was trained how to value and care for them. To consistently and kindly send feedback even if the supplier's proposal was late, incorrect, and way over budget, and how to always be empathetic to their audience, whatever the circumstances. I explained the loneliness many of our freelancer friends might be fighting and that the 'gift' of empathising with that, and making these partners feel part of 'us' short-term, was of critical importance and value. I had seen these principles work in South East Asia and I knew that however deep the cultural specificities were, the human ones are always deeper.

I told the team the story of an occasion in Singapore when we had a client at a large brand who was driving the agency team crazy with his rudeness. One day, one of our directors, a strong and competent force of professional finesse, broke down in tears of fury and considered resigning because of this one client. I could understand her irritation

Emotional contagion, such as laughing when someone else is laughing, proves our empathetic abilities as people are deep rooted. Joy is contagious because empathy allows it to be so.

and absolutely knew why she was angry and hurt, but what I didn't know enough about was the other side of the coin— the client's reality. This was the narrative I began to unpack with her. In order to address the issue, we had to stand in the client's shoes, as emotionally difficult as that might be. It took monumental patience, compression of ego, and a hearty dose of forgiveness, but in my experience, you can never win with anger or by 'fighting fire with fire'. I suggested that perhaps we needed as a team (and with a fair number of tea breaks, chocolate biscuits, and team nights out!) to approach the issue with compassion and to commit to believing that on the whole, even the toughest of clients are not bad people, they are just people dealing with their own baggage.

To this day I train my teams in that fundamental empathetic principle: that there are many more good people than bad, and that people respond to their own realities in their own way but that we should give every situation the breathing room to show its true colours before reacting. Although I wholly disagree with there ever being a need to treat people badly, the opportunity to try and see things through the other person's eyes, to see the world as she or he did when 'in action', is always there for us to embrace.

I remember the director looking at me at the time with some distrust, and a fair amount of frustration (we were early on in our relationship and she was ready to scream), but she told me she would give it a go.

A few months later, the storm was undoubtedly much less tumultuous, and she came to me one day to tell me that our new approach was working and she had actually begun to like her client a whole lot more. Before I knew it, they were going out for lunch together and then one day I heard them on the phone. I could only hear the agency side of the call, but I could hear enough to know that they were not only empathising with each other, they were actually problem solving on each other's behalf. In the end they brought their entire relationship back to life because of the kindness the director was able to show the client, and in reality, the fix was relatively quick. People tend to mirror behaviour, so however hard it is taking the first step to empathising or deeply understanding someone else's motives and reality, in most cases it doesn't take long for the person to start reciprocating. This is the magic of humanity's secret success formula in action. It's advice worth sharing.

PAYING IT FORWARD

I believe that whoever it is that helps you today to do your job (in whatever small way) absolutely deserves to be recognised for that role, and critically, to be recognised with thanks. We simply cannot win wars alone—we need our troops—and it rings true for me that "thank you" is the most underestimated phrase in every language. **In the end, the best bosses across all organisations are the ones people like**, and people like people who look them in the eye and say thank you and mean it! This is simple human decency.

I was clear with my team that the only way to get back on track was to extend our empathetic behaviour externally and to make as many true friends and trusted partners as possible. We needed a credible reputation, which was not something that could be built on shallow behaviour or insincerity. We had to say thank you and mean it, we had to look out for our partners and mean it, and we had to put our own money on the line to prove it. We had to commit to living our human *values* in order to be able to turn around the business value on the back of them. Fundamentally, our culture developed to believe that core to our Empathy Advantage success would be the fact that the more people felt authentically listened to, understood, and recognised, the more likely they were to stay and excel in their performance with us. It comes back to the principle of entrenching the knowledge into all team members that they are working *with* you and not *for* you.

THE SHARP EDGES OF BEING AN EMPATHIC LEADER

I couldn't save everyone, and I lost huge pieces of my soul during the months that followed. Of all empathetic principles, the hardest to master is how to use empathy when making tough decisions that negatively impact others. There comes a time when you have to empathise with the health and wellbeing of a whole group over the individual, and this is a very hard line to draw. In the end I had to have many meetings with team members, all of whom I personally liked and respected, to explain that we had headcount well beyond what the bottom line could handle and why that meant we needed to change for the wider impact of the team and organisation. Without a doubt there are people who find it hard to forgive the choices I had to make. Sadly, we simply didn't have the funds to keep everyone, and I knew that if the money we did have wasn't working 100 percent optimally, I simply couldn't pull us out of the quicksand. It was a hauntingly hard time.

I think being a woman and a mother put me at a disadvantage during those days. Although I totally believe in equality and mutual equity, and that male leaders can and should show maternal tendencies (while

Allowing people to see that they are 'wanted' is the greatest gift a leader can give to a team that has lost its mojo.

female leaders can leverage paternal tendencies), I can't help but think that if I were a man, I would have found a little more peace at the time and that I would have allowed the stones to bounce a little more. Maybe I would have taken the whole thing less personally? Perhaps, perhaps not. Either way, I tried to take the high road, day in and day out, and respect the opinions of others as part of their reality. Every day I took a deep breath and visualised exactly where I wanted us to be, poured another cup of tea, and decided that however low people went, I would choose to focus on the possibility, on what I knew we could achieve. I chose to see the best in everyone at all times. I chose to empathise. It was that belief that brought the lining to every one of the dark clouds. **I let the discomfort be my fire and not my fear.**

DIFFICULT DECISIONS AND DEFINITIVE RESULTS

How do you balance the needs of the individual with the needs of the group and business?

This is where empathetic leadership and decision making becomes a theme that many specialists debate at length. It is where the hard edge of committing to empathy comes alive. Although being an empathetic leader means walking in the shoes of your team, understanding their realities, and working with them to enhance them, there are times when your empathetic compass has to be firmly swung to the macro empathetic impact rather than the compassion or commitment you feel personally for an individual. It is possible to empathise with an individual and still make decisions that they don't like or that impact their reality negatively. As a leader you have to do 'unfair' things in the name of macro impact or a wider circle of influence. People may lose their job or experience bad times due to your decisions, but the difference comes into its own when you can lead and share the reality of those decisions with empathy.

This is where the Empathy Advantage became a compass for me. Taking the time to listen to the reactions, the feedback, and the needs of the person and trying to give those team members the support they needed in the wake of an entirely disruptive and uncomfortable situation was a daily commitment. Extending their pay check, their health insurance, their visa, helping them find another role, widening their network, writing to their landlord, supporting them in fixing their CV… whatever it took, because in the end, people come first and just because they were not right for that particular role didn't mean they wouldn't be perfect for another one. Whatever I did, I didn't hide from the pain. I knew I had to make tough decisions and then own them with heart in order to empathetically be able to influence the greater output.

Earlier in this book, we looked at how the US Army uses empathy in combat situations. Although the corporate world is never quite a war zone, the conversations and processes can feel amazingly like a fight. Another example of empathy's power in the sharpest edges of conflict or change is found in the story of Sue Rahr, the executive director of the Washington State Criminal Justice Training Commission. Sue was responsible for developing a training program designed to move the American policing culture away from what she calls a "warrior mentality" when approaching tough scenarios, and to encourage police officers to view themselves not as the "combatants within a community but as guardians of it."[xlviii] She set to teaching the police force how to protect and serve but with humanity and kindness first. I can only imagine how hard a cultural shift that must have been and it's a continual inspiration to me.

Sue talks about an approach called LEED ("listening and explaining with equity and dignity") that teaches police officers to listen to the citizens they encounter, understand their realities, and use their well-formed police actions to reflect them.[lxix] What makes her approach unique is that she is infiltrating the heart into the minds of the police force; she is educating them that however hard the decision and outcome, there is a way to leverage empathy in moving forward swiftly with that decision. I believe 100 percent that if we can train police leaders to act with empathy in the darkest of criminal environments, we can certainly leverage the same skills in the difficult moments of corporate leadership.

THE SIX LIST

I developed a list of six practices that I knew I could rely on to help drive the turnaround process with humanity above all else. Tough decision making need not mean a lack of respect and decency for the people impacted by the change, and the ***/ix Pist*** became a virtual handbook I carried all day during those long and difficult days.

1. Focus on creating **shared awareness:** Ensure your team is aware of the business journey and reality at all times. Try to never keep secrets from the team as to what you are doing and why (within confidentiality bounds, of course). The more involved they are, the more value they will add.

2. **Always honour honesty:** In the hardest of conversations and the most awkward of meetings, be honest in answering every question that anyone asks. Be honest about timeframes and be honest about the answers you don't have. Transparency creates trust, and trust drives loyalty.

3. **Practise live (empathetic) listening:** Try to listen to every piece of feedback, the direct and the indirect. Write it in a journal, analyse it, and work through what is purely emotional (and therefore not of value beyond the individual) and what could be valuable on a wider level. You will need to make decisions on what to consider as critical and what not to, but commit to hearing everything people want to share—use it or lose it but make sure you hear it.

4. **All decision making should be participatory decision making:** Ensure that key decision making is made with your wider team's participation. There is great value in group think as part of vision and path planning. Ask the team questions and question their answers; it will lead to a deeper source of wisdom.

5. **Never underestimate small gestures, they always matter:** The small and the humble cannot be underestimated.

Showing you care with a thank-you note, a personal call, a handwritten card. These tiny gestures so often mean far more than a grand gesture or even a financial bonus. Whether signage, speech, a memo, or body language, in a world being reshaped by technology, people are affected more than ever by the authentic sense of humanity.

6. **Leave the walls of the office behind:** Conversations about someone's future, especially negative or strained conversations, are better outside the office. Always. A change in environment automatically changes the state of the conversation and its participants. It builds trust and confidentiality into a neutral space and it removes the power structures associated with the office environment. Put yourselves in the shoes of the person you are talking to and work out where a more comfortable space would be. A local coffee shop, a walk in the park, a bar down the street? The ambient noise, the ability to hold the warmth of a coffee cup in their hands, the access to distraction to ease awkward moments, these things all allow a more human and natural conversation. Having life-changing meetings in an office meeting room where people feel others may overhear or walk in creates unnecessary anxiety. Not to mention that the team member may worry about exiting the room, how they look or their composure. Take them away from the heart of the business, give them space, and allow them to feel grounded in the environment around them, then give them the luxury of knowing they can walk away. There is an exit and they have the opportunity to leave that meeting from any direction with time to think. No one ever felt truly comfortable considering life decisions in a corporate meeting room!

When I look at the team's transformation over the course of a few years, I know these tough decisions were right for a business that was otherwise headed for imminent bankruptcy. It's a testament to the team that they flew toward being one of the fastest growing agency teams in the city, winning landmark clients. The phone started to ring and clients wanted to be in the room with our team because we felt different. Our culture stood out. Our transparency was fresh and our commitment was real. Our whole team believed in kindness and empathising with our clients and our consumers and they believed it because they felt it and lived it, and not because they were told to 'sell it'.

The whole experience eventually proved to me that empathy does bring joy and contentedness and that these emotions, when rippled across a team with a clear strategy, builds business, competitive edge, and profit. Faster than one would expect.

Thank goodness for that.

Chapter 13

PEOPLE ABOVE ALL ELSE

The business was doing better, and I was focused entirely on leveraging the Empathy Advantage to continue the upward curve. We had escaped dire straits prior to year-end, but we still had a significant mountain to climb.

As advertising agencies, our businesses grow on the back of our people; on their IP, IQ, and experience. It is ironic then that we so often miss the monumental value of leveraging their EQ and that so many large agencies today have lost their way in terms of putting these treasured beings first. I recently discussed this with a senior HR leader from one of the world's largest agencies in the USA. We fiercely agreed with the fact that agencies are missing out on a huge percent of their people's potential by allowing them and their wellbeing to fall down the list of priorities. She shared the following anecdote with me.

The agency had a senior leader in the team who was systematically making people unhappy within the agency, one by one. Younger members were resigning and teams were crumbling. This was not a secret; in fact, this woman's behaviour was impacting people so much that the wider industry knew of her (word spreads fast). Rumour has it that she had even had a job offer revoked when the middle management of a new business heard she was on her way. The surprising thing is that the original agency in question is a reputable and successful agency that values culture and their people, so this equation felt really out of place. Why would this scenario be allowed to occur and why was no one doing anything about it? I pushed the HR lead to explain why they would keep this employee even though it was well documented that she was an unfair and unkind leader. The answer was both simple and simply devastating: "The client liked her."

I know, I know, it's not new, right?

But have our businesses really lost track of what's truly of value? For as long as we live in fear of our clients walking out, we can never truly listen to, or empathise with, our teams. We will make bad decisions. The colossal Empathy Gap between the people we hire and the people that pay us will soon be far too wide for any corporate surgeon or leadership coach to stitch back together. Your clients can never be more important that your own assets.

I am not naïve. I have run large agency brands and I know what the margin pressures are and how demanding your biggest clients can be. I have held clients that I knew were not entirely aligned culturally with our own, and there were times when, in order to protect people's salaries in the short term, I got caught off guard keeping a client when probably we shouldn't have. There are times when you temporarily have to maintain client relationships that you rather wouldn't, but the key is that as leaders we can do this in a way that ensures our own teams are never truly compromised, and that they never feel you would choose the client's reality over the team's own wellbeing.

As a small business we have both more and less power where this is concerned. Less because we are always one large client away from disaster (!), but more because we have more holistic control to say no. There are fewer senior stakeholders mandating what we can and can't do, and there are fewer repercussions when we do say no and remove a client. There have been many times when I have explained to our wider

"LEADERS PUT PEOPLE FIRST."

SIMON SINEK

leadership team that we cannot, or will not, take a client, however big the potential cheque, because my instinct or 'gut' tells me they are not a fit. This can be received with great frustration because instinct is deeply personal and an entirely non-scaleable skill, but it is often, in my experience, the greatest tool you have as a leader. The more confident I grow in my role and career, the better I use this tool, and today I trust my core response more than any other 'provable' or measurable fact. What is on paper can never be of more value than what you feel in a room when you meet someone, or when you watch their behaviour toward others.

I remember one key occasion when we had a really exciting new business pitch. The client was a fantastic e-com start-up, and we went into the presentation alive with energy. The presentation was compelling, in fact it was brilliant, and we had a team of really smart specialists in the room. Sadly, the key client seemed not to think so, but not because she listened to it and decided there were better partners out there, but because she never put her cell phone down to take any of it in. She sat there for the whole pitch glued to her phone screen, flying through content that was clearly infinitely more important than we were. I cannot think of anything more disrespectful or rude after two weeks of work and the massive amounts of passion we had poured into her brand.

As the client team left that day, we closed the meeting room door behind them and stood for a moment looking at each other in bemused silence. We knew instantly that our culture and beliefs couldn't forgive her behaviour and that we didn't want to work with them. More importantly, after everything we had promised our team in terms of our values and culture meant we couldn't work with them, whatever the upside. We emailed them a few hours later saying that unfortunately we didn't think we would be a fit for what they were looking for. It was empowering and it probably created more energy, cohesion, and momentum in our team than a win would have!

A month or so later we did the same with another start-up that also looked creatively full of potential but didn't deliver on any of the human fundamentals we were committed to, even in the initial communications. In both cases the clients wrote back asking us to reconsider, but we stood firm that the disconnect was on a deeper level than an email could fix. This wasn't about ego; it was about heart and about finding clients who put human decency and respect into the centre of every room.

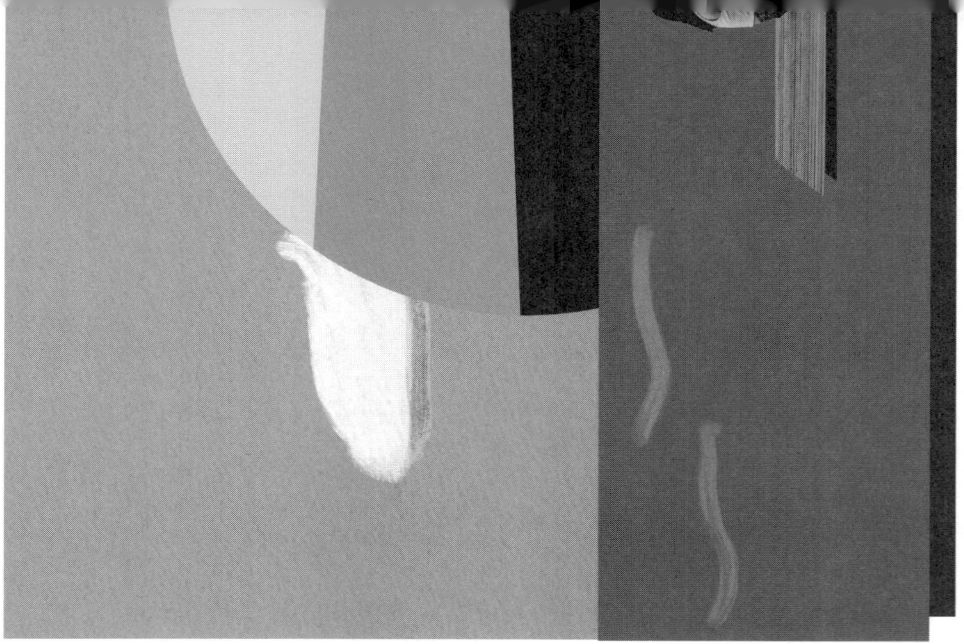

Chapter 14

THE TURNING OF PARASYMPATHETIC COGS

At a fundamental level, as human beings, we are all the same. Cultures, habits, and lifestyle aside, all of us aspire for happiness and none of us want to suffer. We may have created a very shiny world for ourselves, of affluence and of consumption of the 'things' all around us, but just beneath that surface there is something else bubbling. It's a negative bubbling and it pulls us together into a shared and often painful reality. It's viscous and it doesn't discriminate against who it impacts. Stress.

Like the heavy fog that appears at speed to a shore, stress is a silent body of emotional heaviness that sneaks in without us noticing until we suddenly realise we can no longer see our hands in front of our eyes. Stress is a kind of mental unrest that is like a petulant child, nagging and nagging at us until we eventually explode into a deluge of turmoil and the words *"I need time out"* are ringing out all over the city.

When you hear the term 'social welfare' you may instinctively think about government social services or protecting children and the disadvantaged from neglect and strain, but perhaps social welfare from 2020 onward should hold a much wider lens and look at the corporate neglect that companies around the world are inflicting on their citizens? Burnout, health issues (high blood pressure, heart disease, obesity, diabetes), reliance on drugs or alcohol, detachment from society, and even suicide are social evils that we are increasingly accepting of. I can't help but wonder, though, that if we saw an entire species of animals, say a herd of elephants, doing a similar thing to their own species, we would probably make headline news about it. There would be a National Geographic expedition to immediately help the herd stop the self-abuse destroying the group and a crowdfunding campaign would begin for animal welfare intervention. We would stop the rot. Yet, amongst our own tribe this lack of respect for the struggle of our people and our own social environment appears to be gathering speed downhill, without the mass intervention it deserves. The deluge of cyberbullying and social abuse that occurs today is only one signal that the impact of this ever-present stress on our empathetic abilities is causing ruptures in society.

In earlier chapters I have unpacked the increasing recognition, and growing body of science, that confirms the connection between our state of mind and state of health. If our corporate lives continue to entrench the levels of detachment we see today, and we remain in a state of stress and strain permanently, civilization will suffer. It's that simple. The one thing we humans so consistently try to avoid—suffering—is something we are incrementally and conscientiously driving daily.

Yet the solution to a better world of work is not complex. It is as simple as committing to transforming our working worlds to a place where people are happier. This was a clear goal for me as I continued to drive our 'Happiest Agency' agenda. Creating a commonplace practice of listening, of caring, and of empathising, with a methodology that balanced humanism with the capitalist practices we rely on, was firmly on our agenda as a wider team. It is our gift as humans to be able to use our intelligence and capacity for compassion to address this cycle and preserve our health by hitting refresh. The question is why aren't we doing this more consistently?

REFRESHING PERSPECTIVES

"We have come here to let the world leaders know that change is coming whether you like it or not." [lxx] These were the words of fifteen-year-old Greta Thunberg at the COP 24 Climate Conference in 2019, and they became instantly famous. She was talking specifically about climate change, but her word represents the attitudes of her generation. Today's youth are entering adulthood confident that they can and will build a better future for themselves. Case studies from all over the world, gathered by the World Youth Report (from the UN) in 2019, confirm that young people's optimism about this is unabated.[lxxi] This optimism and commitment to change often focuses on the outputs of our society—sustainability agendas, environmental balance, gender equality, and the rights of the less abled—but the inputs, our stress levels, our mental health, our emotional intelligence, and our norms for social cohesion, of which empathy is one metric at its core, will gather increasing momentum. The younger members of our workforce, of

your workforce, see things very differently, and exhaustion and stress are no longer accepted as standard byproducts of 'working hard.'

In my own leadership journey, my yoga training supports my belief that we can all take a proactive approach to reducing stress within our teams. Stress is something that builds over time, but reducing it can happen quite quickly if you set your mind, and your corporate culture, to doing so. As my Empathy Advantage strategy deepened its influence, I created my own approach to stress reduction in those months. **I called it the Parasympathetic Cogs.**

The idea is to give the team a chance for a total reset, emotionally and physically, by putting into action a series of cogs. Each cog seems small, but when actioned together, they can turn around the energy and stress levels. Data from the University of Warwick in the UK found that happy people are 12 percent more productive, and an even deeper set of studies by the Queens School of Business and by the Gallup Organization showed that stressed and disengaged workers had a 37 percent higher rate of absenteeism, 49 percent more accidents and 60 percent higher chance of errors, as well as 18 percent lower productivity, 16 percent lower profitability, 37 percent lower job growth, and **65 percent lower share price over time.**[lxxii] Reversing stress isn't only the right thing to do, it's the profitable thing to do.

These stress-to-life connectors are of deep relevance to me as a leader and were the reason I trained to become a yoga teacher and Ayurvedic therapist in the first place. Fundamentally, the science behind these yogic specialisms looks at the impact of our limbic system and the sympathetic nervous system (our high-stress, fight or flight mode) and how we can reduce them for a better state of health and wellbeing. The opposite state to this stress-driven sympathetic nervous system is called the parasympathetic nervous system and it is the state we reside in when we are not stressed. When we are relaxed, at peace and going about our days as humanity intended; fully functioning, optimally healthy, and fuelled for success. The yogic science behind the nervous system dates back much further than any of the research studies aforementioned in this book; it was originally founded by Patanjali prior to 400 CE. It is truly ancient thinking.[lxxiii] Whether you subscribe to yoga or not,

"HAPPINESS IS THE MEANING AND THE PURPOSE OF LIFE, THE WHOLE AIM AND END OF HUMAN EXISTENCE."

ARISTOTLE

whether you love it or hate it, yogic science is based on how humans have evolved to respond to stress on a hormonal level, and many of our medical systems today reflect these principles. What we know is that the estimated cost of stress-related conditions (in 2018) was a cost on the US healthcare system alone of an estimated k300 billion.[lxxiv] It is a debilitating problem economically, socially, and financially in many markets worldwide. As human beings we simply weren't made for this level of stress and it is costing us, and our governments, an unimaginable amount of money and resources to manage.

To gauge the extent of this impact, a large review of seventy academic studies looked at the association between positive wellbeing and longevity in both healthy people and those with a pre-existing health condition, such as heart or kidney disease. Their results showed that a higher positive wellbeing/happiness index was found to have a favourable effect on survival, reducing the risk of early death by 18 percent in healthy people and by 2 percent in those with pre-existing disease.[lxxv] When we consider this in the context of a Cisco report in 2019 that shows that over 87 percent of employees worldwide say they suffer from stress in the workplace, and that left unmanaged, this stress will seriously impact a person's physical health and wellbeing, we can see the direct link between health and our 'wealth' as businesses and people.[lxxvi] Stress is well known to lead to higher levels of absenteeism and a lack of productivity, and according to a study by the *Journal of Occupational Health Psychology*, can cost businesses up to k187 billion per year (2015).[lxxvii] Within an organisational context, beyond the absenteeism or lack of productivity, the wider impact is that people are so busy reacting to stress and feeling reactive, irritable, or uncomfortable that they are not able to switch on the higher order, more emotive part of the brain, the prefrontal cortex. This part of the brain would enable them to improve awareness, perspective, and optimal levels of EQ and teamwork, so when it is missing it directly impacts people's ability to connect and work together. Put simply, when people are very stressed they cannot focus on others and therefore they definitely cannot empathise. The impact is that as the business environment becomes more and more stressful, and our ability to support each other becomes lower and lower, a vicious circle commences. You can immediately see how the last three decades of high corporate stress and strain have been negatively building into the types of cultures and leadership styles we are seeing today. The more stressed the leaders have been, the less they have been able to empathise and connect with those around them. And so it continues and manifests into the teams and structures around them.

An empathy gap that fuelled a further empathy gap!

TURNING THE COGS

In early 2019, I found myself wondering why we couldn't implement a parasympathetic yet high performing system into our workplace, just like yoga teaches its students to. If the parasympathetic nervous system puts us into a state of being stress free, and we can therefore function to our full potential, it follows that we can incrementally improve happiness and performance in equal measure if we can activate a low stress environment more often. My goal was to ensure that we were implementing ways to turn off the sympathetic nervous system (fighting or flighting) and instead activating this opposite system, responsible for calming us and reconnecting us with reality. I knew that in so doing we would be allowing team members to connect with each other and build a cohesive unit, whilst improving output simultaneously and softening the edges of the day-to- day working environment.

This goal was like a fire burning inside me, for three key reasons. Firstly, because I really wanted people to be happy. I had learnt during my time in Singapore that this was my ultimate driver in both my professional and personal life, as well as obviously being the ultimate goal of all employees. Secondly, because I know that happiness is contagious and that essentially, happy people make other people happy. (Step away from the miserable ones and surround yourself with glass-half-full people and it absolutely will change your outlook and that of those around you.) And thirdly, because as a businessperson, I knew that contented, emotionally strong, and fulfilled people make business sense. They make more money. They work longer hours with more focus, by choice. There are endless examples of how motivated, fulfilled people are more productive and more innovative, not to mention the fact that clients are drawn to those who love their jobs. I knew that a team of happy people will always be able to tick the boxes of both profit and purpose, and that people who feel seen, understood, and valued make more money. The Global Empathy Index in the USA suggests that "empathic cultures significantly impact the financial performance of a company" and shows that the top ten empathetic businesses in the index generated 50 percent more income than the bottom ten in 2016.[lxxvii]

The cost of my goals was not altogether easy to execute when we were still fighting a monumental battle to stabilise the ship financially, and I had very little flexibility as to what I could implement and at what pace. I decided therefore to implement a series of small and low-cost commitments that would either have a direct and short-term impact on stress levels, or an indirect impact on future stress levels, by making the team feel more in control, more valued, and more secure about their future. One of the first of these commitments was to buy a Bluetooth speaker and start playing music every day. The first cog in action.

THE SOUND OF MUSIC

I wanted to leverage the power of sound to bring energy into the office environment. This act allowed me to ask people to play their own favourites from their own countries, which got the conversation rolling around some hotly debated music choices, and the sound was able to change the feeling of the room at any given time. There were some very entertaining tracks that popped up, and the stories behind them certainly started to stir up the humanity that was bubbling in this eclectic group of people. I learnt to never underestimate the power of sound (something I also learned from yoga) and the ability of sound to change a room or environment instantly. If people choose to wear headphones or need to go to a quiet space, that's absolutely OK, but the greater impact of having music unite a room or office, from the minute people arrive in the morning, is absolutely worth the drawbacks of anyone moaning about not wanting to hear that track again. It was equally a very powerful strategy in changing the way clients, and even senior leaders, perceived the office when they walked in; the music quite literally started to change our culture.

George Eliot once said: *"There is no feeling... that does not find relief in music"* and I think she was absolutely right.[lxxix] In large client meetings, workshops, or team brainstorms, we still pay great attention to sound. I have seen first-hand across all markets how music can make the difference between a successful meeting and a less successful one. Whatever your culture, music is a great human unifier. It opens people up to approving concepts, it helps people feel brave enough to buy new ideas or make a higher investment than they were planning. It levels the ground amongst layers of teams and clients. Psychologists have found that listening to music in fact 'lights up' whole areas of the brain associated with a complex set of emotions and therefore has the magic power of tapping into our instinctive, emotional triggers.[lxxx] Interestingly, a 2018 study by the Southern Methodist University, Dallas, and UCLA showed that people with higher empathy actually process familiar music with greater involvement of the reward system in the brain, the areas responsible for processing social information.[lxxxi]

What this study concluded was that music is deeply related to how we process the social world and the environment we are in and therefore how that environment affects our brain and our response to it. Additionally, I remember reading once that a Swedish electronics store found that customers on average spent eight more minutes in the store, resulting in a 78 percent increase in sales, when music was playing in the background.[lxxxii] Music is about humans interacting with other humans and communicating with each other, triggering the same processes at work in the brain that are at play during social interactions. Music aids how we interact and behave so it can play a hugely important role in creating an empathetically driven organisation and reducing pressure. Such a simple step to reducing stress levels and changing the dynamic of our team and client connectivity.

BEYOND THE MUSIC

Once we were sitting as a united team, and the tracks were playing, the next thing was to look at our HR principles to make sure the team felt cared for and protected in the life- impacting areas of their roles. We committed to close the office during certain holidays throughout the year to ensure people got more time off to supplement their annual leave. We agreed to close the office at year-end, even though the local market has no official leave, to acknowledge global festive periods important to many of the team. We did performance appraisals with every team member for the first time, allowing them to share their goals and drivers and formally listening to how they would like to see the company roll out in the coming months. And we changed our health insurance policy to give them globally recognised coverage that was a market leader in benefits, creating a sense of care and attention to both them and their loved ones.

As part of this Parasympathetic Cogs process, we also sent out an anonymous survey asking the team what we could do to improve their working environment and their wellbeing in the workplace. To my absolute joy we had full responses from everyone for the first time ever. The act of being asked was a first for them, and as I had hoped, they jumped at the chance to find their voices and opinions. We implemented nearly every idea that the team had, which included:

1. A better coffee machine. Funnily enough, this was a resounding winner across the board! We invested in a fantastic machine and started providing fresh milk for coffee. Such a simple fix.
2. Better seating arrangements to improve natural light and space in the office. More on this in chapter 15.
3. Giving everyone their birthday off and replacing the meaningless balloon that had previously been tied to their chair on the big day with a food order of their choice the day before or after for the team to share, bringing the wonder of multicoloured donuts, karak chai, and cupcakes to the office frequently.
4. Replacing fake plants with as many real ones as possible.
5. Creating comfortable seating areas and getting more beanbags.
6. Providing gym membership to the corporate gym.
7. Team building events throughout the year.
8. Fresh fruit, daily fruit-infused water, and treats throughout the week; small sparks to brighten the day.
9. Better music!
10. Redecoration of the office, which it turned out none of them liked or felt any connection with, so a fresh look was definitely needed.
11. A more welcoming reception area.
12. Better IT and server system and a host of other functional requirements for email, Wi-Fi, and hard drives.

None of these things alone are at all mind-opening, but the implementation of them as a response to actively talking to the team about enjoying work more and offering interventions that understood their reality was incredibly powerful. It reflected Regenerative Leadership at its core by putting inclusivity and equity for our shared journey at the outset of the regeneration and allowed them to choose exactly how they wanted to spend their working hours. It created a ripple effect.

One of the final steps was to redecorate and re-energise the working environment. This represents a huge part of activating a lower stress inducing environment. The Spanish philosopher José Ortega y Gasset once said: *"I am I, plus my surroundings; and if I do not preserve the latter, I do not preserve myself."*[lxxxiii]

Empathetic team environments have to start with the environment itself. I knew instinctively that the working environment was deeply connected with lower stress levels and that core to the success of the Parasympathetic Cogs would be to restructure the space and redecorate.

As an extremely considered (and very tight budgeted!) design adventure began, the cogs of our new system were turning.

Chapter 15

THE INEXTRICABLE MAGIC BETWEEN PEOPLE AND PLACE

As I developed my Parasympathetic Cog approach further, I began to ask myself why it is that so many working environments aren't more comfortable. Is there any reason why the office that we spend our days in can't become our very own *village* that integrates the team into a shared, and cared for, environment? If we look again to evolution to guide us, the space we share as social groups has always been very impactful on our ability to progress. Since the beginning of time, humans have been innately sensitive to their surroundings, both for survival and for comfort.[lxxxiv] We seek out environments that ooze the qualities we feel at ease in, environments that reflect who we are. Just look at the amount of attention and money people spend perfecting their homes! So, why is it that office design is so often done for external appearances and not for those who actually work within the business? An environment that reflects the people engaging in the space is not only empathetically powerful but also just common sense. At its simplest, people will thrive in an environment that better understands, and therefore suits, their needs.

I knew our experience of our workspace would be deeply impactful on our relationships, as well as our wellbeing, and that it would therefore have a direct impact on performance and output. The space I set out to create was based on this philosophy, and although its flex had to be tightened given our budget was pretty much zero, I set about finding as many ways around this as possible. Where there is a will there is a way!

PAINT COLOURS AND PRODUCTIVITY

A few weekends later, there we were, wandering the halls of IKEA, the Chinese mega mall, and discount stores citywide. The shared shopping experience itself became quite the entertainment in the weeks that followed, as we knocked down walls, put a window from reception through to the rest of the office, and put in a new meeting room. We reversed the direction of our conference room and put in a statement wall, a new set of décor, and even some pink flamingos! The movement of the TV screen from one end of the room to the other, along with the new décor, created the feeling of an entirely new space,

"HUMANS AND THE ENVIRONMENT HAVE BEEN INTERACTING SINCE HUMANS FIRST WALKED THE EARTH. HUMANS CHANGE THEIR ENVIRONMENT BOTH POSITIVELY AND NEGATIVELY AND THE ENVIRONMENT AFFECTS ALL AREAS OF HUMAN BEHAVIOUR AND LIFE..."

OPRAH WINFREY

at a very small budget. The new meeting room was packed out with fake grass, comfortable sofas and a coffee table with space for fresh flowers and fairy lights, and a statement 'film director's' lamp brought a glow to the entire space. We opened up the existing long wooden desks, creating space for more people around the large pine workspaces, and stripped the walls back from the crazy concoction of legacy designs to a fresh and bright off white that immediately created more light and gave us more of a brand consultancy energy than the forced "we are trying to be creative" feel that had been donning the walls beforehand. Fresh new cushions featuring palm tree leaves and exotic flowers arrived and the team had a spring in their step. They truly felt their opinions and needs were being reflected in the design and the new energy it had created, and if there had ever been an empathetic interior project, this was it. We planned every corner to meet the desires of our people and nothing else. There was a notable air of celebration!

The response from the team as they arrived in the days following the work was phenomenal. As the light flew in, and the new bowls of fresh fruit and chocolate arrived, the energy jumped a fair few rungs up the ladder we were on. Stress levels were quite obviously lowering. They didn't disappear overnight, of course, but the design, plus the true heart and energy behind its intention, was working its magic.

THE KNOCK-ON EFFECT OF KNOCKING DOWN WALLS

Although we didn't design for anyone but ourselves, our clients were surprised by the new look, and even today it is common for new clients to comment on how much they enjoy being in the space. It must be due to the true care and personalised passion that went into every piece, because in itself the design is far from breakthrough. There is something deeper to the connection people feel to it, and I think that it is the heart behind its creation that people connect with. It has meant that on multiple occasions, clients who had previously not stepped into the agency at all, have asked us to host them at our new offices in the new space. Not only was this always an absolute honour and joy for

"OUR INTERIORS ARE AN INSIGHT INTO OUR BRAINS. IT IS A COLLABORATION OF DESIGN, ART, HUMOR, IRONY AND FUNCTIONALITY."

AMANDA TALBOT, RETHINK: THE WAY YOU LIVE

the team, because they truly had begun to see the clients' valuing us and what our team could offer, but it created financial benefit because we began to be asked to host workshops, which came with significant strategic planning work to support. I remember one particular occasion when we had a senior leader from Samsung say that she would like her home to look like our offices! The pride amongst the team was firmly set and we all beamed. In every new compliment, our shared ownership of what we had created became a deeper connection point between all of those who worked within its walls. The impact of the redesign was much wider than just our shared physical surroundings though; it represented fresh beginnings, new expectations, and mutual respect as a group within a context that people actively wanted to care for, as well as share. All the trends of the 'sharing economy' were visible, people were thriving in the space, but we were equally bringing to life a newer and more impactful caring economy of our own, one where the entire team felt more connected to each other as well as our new space. The *ripple* effect was firmly in action and the (tiny!) investment in the design of the office had created new revenue streams, as well as new hope for our team.

Wider changes going on in the holding group meant there was one area I couldn't implement as planned at the time, and that was the Meditation Room. This was a real shame because I felt confident that for the tiny space it needed, the benefit in terms of our emotional agility levels was bound to have been significant. The ability to give people space to remove themselves, to think, to be alone with themselves or simply silent, would have been greatly beneficial.

The final investment was into three aromatherapy diffusers. I had started working on ensuring we had a set of scents specifically chosen each week to aid in the wellbeing of the team at that particular time. The use of scent is widely used in the corporate and retail worlds to specifically change the feeling of a room and the behaviour of those who enter it. Although entirely subliminal, the leverage of scent in our office would be another key part of the turnaround. The team accepted it with some trepidation, but within weeks it became a staple and I often emailed in those early months about the scents I was mixing that week and why. We had scents to uplift, freshen up, or energise, or if there was a late-night pitch, a scent to keep us all alert. Again, I suspect the actual scents themselves were just one part, powerful as scent is, and that the overriding empathetic influence was simply the act itself. The fact that they felt their leader was investing personally and passionately into all areas of the team's wellbeing, and was committed to creating happiness and stability wherever possible, changed their view of leadership. The scents remained a staple in our office, and clients and visitors alike still comment on it often. Not only did we look better and feel better, but we smelt better too!

Chapter 16

INSTINCT OVER INSIGHT

For many months I asked myself every day, *do I expose my heart?*

My teams would tell you that I am heart-driven, but it took *many* many years for me to get comfortable with the concept of baring my heart. Finding the confidence to use it as a strength openly was the hardest role I ever took on. It can be an incredibly scary thing to do, and demands always- on endurance, composure, and diligence. Anyone who thinks doing so is using a 'soft' skill has clearly never tried it.

Leading with heart is the move from leading with only your rational business intelligence to leading with emotional intelligence and intuition. It requires a balance of our analytical intelligence and emotional intelligence. As leaders, we can look at sets of data and spreadsheets for days, but we risk missing out on the bigger picture, the intuitive understanding of our businesses, if we are looking for rational insight alone. Leading with heart is not a soft skill saved for yogic retreats or the education industry. Contrary to some opinion, no empathetic leader could ever be defined as a 'pushover' or too 'gentle' because the energy, fortitude, and grit that you have to preserve (often behind the scenes) to be this kind of leader is monumental. It is a Regenerative Leadership commitment that sees you practising with a truly conscious focus on the potential and wellbeing of your people, and it is far tougher to lead with heart than it is to do the opposite.

As the CEO of Microsoft and *Financial Times* Person of the Year 2019, Satya Nadella, states: *"Now the challenge, is that you can't just say 'I'll go to work and turn on my empathy.' I'm not claiming that empathy is innate, it is something that needs to be developed."*[lxxxv]

An empathetic leader is not always someone who leads with heart, however someone who can bring empathy and leadership into coexistence, whilst mastering anger, disappointment, and impatience, to be able to continually create a culture where people feel valued, cared for, and encouraged to perform will find that a heart-led approach comes more easily. These leaders commit to aligning people's wellbeing and needs with business decision making on an ongoing basis, and this adds an unimaginable amount of pressure to that leader. It can occasionally slow things down, complicate scenarios, and open up your business to the ever- messy journey of the human spirit, but without

"THE JOB OF LEADERSHIP TODAY IS NOT JUST TO MAKE MONEY. IT'S TO MAKE MEANING."

JOHN SEELY BROWN, XEROX PARC

it we are continually fuelling the emotional and connectivity deficit, the Empathy Deficit, behind so many of our wider social and personal issues. Heart-led leadership is a commitment that, when all is said and done, should come with all leadership roles to some extent, whatever type of leader you see yourself to be. After all, you get paid to carry this pressure, to work out how to trust your instinct over insight, and to put empathy ahead of Excel for the benefit of the entire organisation and its people. That is why you have the job and someone else doesn't.

Research in 2016 of over fifteen thousand leaders across three hundred companies in eighteen countries over a ten-year period, from the global leadership development firm DDI, ranked empathy as the number one performing leadership skill in global leaders today. Their research reported that leaders who master empathy perform more than 40 percent higher in coaching their teams, engaging others, and impactful decision making.[lxxxvi]

As time went on in my new role, our revenue doubled and then tripled and I grew in conviction in answering my own question about leading with heart. My conclusion was that if you truly want to grow a business at speed, with vast changes on the bottom line whilst having no detrimental impact to the people in your organisation, then there is probably no other way than to put your heart on the line and out in the open. Our turnaround story felt like an almost impossible success, and I had absolute certainty that it was the team's response to, and uptake of, my own empathetic influence that got us there. I learnt that **a huge part of maintaining this was based in everlasting patience.** Patience to listen, patience to give teams the room to breathe and to learn, and patience to put people beyond performance even when that took longer and more resources. (And of course, the patience not to relook the P&L weekly!)

Tom Gartland, the former President of Avis Budget Group North America, released a book in 2018 named *Lead with Heart*, which soon became a bestseller for these very reasons. Tom's book tells the story of how he put heart at the core of the Avis philosophy and proved that employees who feel valued generate exceptional profits and drove Avis to see significant increase in their bottom line and overall growth performance.[lxxxvii]

As Avis also saw, **in order to unlock the true potential in people, they need to see you, to know you, and to trust you.** None of those things are possible if you lead with your head alone and put up a front or a reflection of who you hope the professional world sees you to be. **You need to mean what you say and say what you mean and deliver on what you promise.**

Demotivation comes from the top, so be under no illusion, if your people aren't happy or performing at their best, you are a significant part of the why. Authenticity is everything. When teams see their leader behaving openly and honestly, they are far more likely to follow them, not because they need to, but because they want to. As I look back at our own turnaround journey, I can pen a set of six behaviours that were deeply associated with how we entrenched this type of leadership.

1. Consistent transparency to build trust that endures the test of time.
2. A commitment to putting value of people, hearing them and seeing them, above vanity or ego, always.
3. Deep belief in stopping the organisation from ever becoming self-seeking but instead driven by the belief in their team and

the building of others. (Critically this was even in the face of a potential, short-term, revenue drop.)

4. Dedication to forgiveness as an emotional strength high on the agenda. Often not seen as a business philosophy, being able to forgive and move forward is key to building trust and to maintaining your own momentum as a leader.
5. Always standing up for what is ethically right or valuable from a humanist point of view, above and beyond the macro business picture at any given time. This one is far easier said than done!
6. Total perseverance on an individual level to allow your team and your leaders to dream, to grow, to fail, and to regenerate.

CONNECTING THE HEART WITH EMOTIONALLY INTELLIGENT LEADERSHIP

One of the unfair ironies of our long careers (that we spend years committing to, to evolve our experience and skillsets) is that the technical skills that got you to leadership in the first place are suddenly of much less importance when you have a tribe of people looking to you to fulfil much more than the act of doing the job every day. This is why we so often hear stories about highly skilled executives who get promoted to top leadership roles and fail or, the opposite, average technically skilled people who manage to fly to new heights when they are given a leadership role. According to *Harvard Business Review*, 71 percent of employers surveyed by CareerBuilder in 2019 said they value EQ over IQ, and yet so often this is a skill no one teaches or trains anyone on.[lxxxviii] The *Harvard Business Review* article commented that employees with high emotional intelligence are more likely to stay calm under pressure, resolve conflict effectively, and respond to co-workers with empathy.[lxxxix] Today, emotional intelligence is truly something that sets people apart, and it is this ability to read and understand the emotions of those around you that allows a leader to deeply connect and influence performance. According to the same article, and quoting a recent survey by the Society for Human Resource Management, 72 percent of employees ranked "respectful treatment of all employees

---

The biggest risk facing leaders today is that we lose touch with our soul.

---

at all levels" as their top factor in job satisfaction. As ever, it does seem pretty obvious that all people really want is to be treated well and respected as the individuals they are.

The delivery of truly leading with heart, with people's best interest above all else, is a multifaceted approach to 'being' in the office every day. It is not simply the commitment to placing the highest leadership order on emotional intelligence, and nor does it end when you put this into words or action, but it infiltrates every living thought about your role and your nonverbal communication. It can be pretty exhausting, to be honest, but the impact of paying attention to open body language, eye contact, and tone of voice is the only way to holistically deliver on this leadership style. These skills are so often lost as our days fly by in a flurry of emails and conference calls, and the opportunity to truly assess other people's emotional states dwindles. When we have large sets of people working from home and via video screens, the requirement for the focus on these physical facets, particularly over a video screen, double in importance.

It has become acceptable, and commonplace, to deliver all kinds of bad or stressful news to people over WhatsApp or email but **make no mistake, an emoji can never be a sign of empathy,** however many smileys or covered-eyed monkeys you add, and however softly you word the message. Speaking in person with your team is the only way to deliver on a consistently emotionally valuable relationship. In our plight to always improve efficiency, to streamline meetings into a Slack chat, and reduce the number of planes we jump on for face-to-face meetings, we must keep one constant in mind: our species thrives

"THE MOST EFFECTIVE LEADERS ARE ALL ALIKE IN ONE CRUCIAL WAY: THEY ALL HAVE A HIGH DEGREE OF WHAT HAS COME TO BE KNOWN AS EMOTIONAL INTELLIGENCE. IT'S NOT THAT IQ AND TECHNICAL SKILLS ARE IRRELEVANT. THEY DO MATTER, BUT... THEY ARE THE ENTRY- LEVEL REQUIREMENTS FOR EXECUTIVE POSITIONS."

DANIEL GOLEMAN, PSYCHOLOGIST

when we connect. No efficiency measures will be as sustainable or powerful as empowering and inspiring the minds, and hands, that work together in harmony to deliver exceptional and surprising performance and creativity.

LOST IN TRANSLATION

Lost in translation is real and not just a 2003 film title! Academic Kitaro Nishida claimed that "*with every conversation, a form of empathy is being used to interpret subtle cues, intentions and emotions*".[xci] We cannot read people's emotions if we can't see them! Over a text-based messaging app or an email, people have selective hearing, they only take in the parts they want to read or remember, and their takeaway is entirely dependent on their own state of mind at the moment they read the message. Content and messages do get lost in translation. Face to face, the conversation can be tailored to ensure the messaging stays on track and can be acted on productively, whether that's via a video call, or ideally in person. As the Zulus believe, the ability to really see people in conversation is to truly recognise their humanity and their importance.

Making the effort to invest in your audience never fails to offer a return. Next time you meet with your team, your boss, or your client, spend an extra second or two to specifically notice their eye colour. You will see just how a touch more connection, of effort to truly notice them and their eyes, makes a massive difference to your conscious ability to be present, as well as their response. People really do react differently when you consciously connect with their eyes and really 'see' them. Empathetic leadership relies on many facets, but you can be sure that leading with your heart often starts with your eyes.

The biggest risk we see facing leadership today is that we lose touch with our soul in place of entirely becoming our role. Leadership can no longer be defined as a mainly rational area of expertise. Popular theory and experience now prove the value of **combining cognition and emotion for improved output.** Where leaders were once taught to keep a "professional distance" and to "avoid getting personal" with their teams, we are now seeing a time when **'being' is significantly valued over the 'doing'.**

The workforce today no longer looks up to leaders who simply do what their job description outlines: they are looking to them to 'be' something to them. To be connected, to be of value, to be in service (as a mentor, coach or friend), and to allow emotional cohesion and connection to flourish.

Organisations by definition are living organisms; they grow, fluctuate, and change. Those organisations with teams that are able to flex, show vulnerability, and openly communicate across areas of complexity are the ones that are able to grow and overcome the deepest of challenging times.

The teams of today crave connection and authenticity, they want to be cared for, they demand engagement in their work beyond the superficial, and **they are looking for significance over success**. The move to leading with heart, or at the very least building humanity into your leadership skill, is no longer an option. It's a prerequisite.

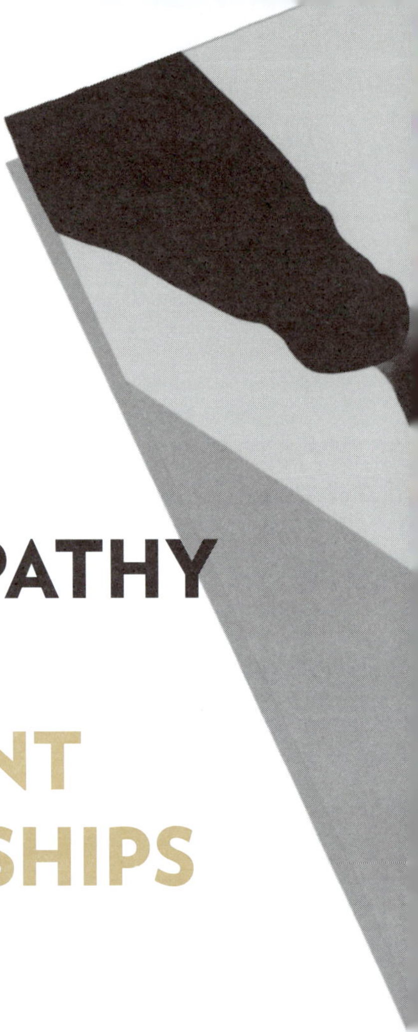

Chapter 17

USING EMPATHY TO BUILD DEEP CLIENT RELATIONSHIPS

There is a lot written about listening skills and the need for leaders to listen; however, far too often we forget what the **true role of listening is, which is to increase our capacity for understanding.**

In organisations everywhere, people are asking questions to gain information instead of garner understanding, and this is a fundamental miss in our corporate culture and training methodologies. After all, you can't expect people to be more connected and cohesive as a team or with their clients if they haven't yet worked out the basics of listening.

Curiosity drives understanding. At its core, one of the simplest ways to understand someone is to ask them a question. The key, of course, is to actually hear the answer. Being heard is a fundamental human motivator and it offers us the ability to transfer information in a mutually beneficial way, allowing us to share context. This sounds so obvious, but the reality is that most leaders are not very good at listening. It may be because they are used to always being the one listened to, it may be due to ego, or it may be because they simply don't care, but whatever the reason, it ever deepens the detached leadership plaguing our industries. This lack of true listening is incredibly demotivating, and what happens over time is that people stop speaking and stop sharing, which is a monumental risk to our businesses and our creativity.

As I write, a senior leader in my circle comes to mind. In many ways this person is a very strong leader and respected by many, but I often wonder whether I am the only person who struggles to hold a conversation with them. Common sense tells me it can't just be me, yet I wonder why no one else is talking about the issue. Have you ever met someone who makes "hmm, hm hm, hmmm" noises as a *constant* accompaniment to your narrative? Well, this leader does that. All the time. Not only does it show that the person is not listening at all, but it is also incredibly distracting and impolite. The monotonous sound effects that the listener believes gives the impression that they are present, are actually the biggest giveaway that your content is of no value to them whatsoever. Over time, what happens? The speaker, or the teams around them, stop talking. After all, if the overriding takeaway is that the conversation is of no value to the leader (and therefore to the speaker) why waste our time? Pretending to want to listen is far worse than not listening at all. Sadly, this isn't uncommon and there are large amounts of self-censorship going on out there as teams halt their sharing, in the fear or frustration that their leaders aren't listening to them.

Studies looking at interactions between those in power and those in less powered positions have shown that the mere act of the person in the higher power position actively seeking the perspective of the lower powered person can significantly enlighten both parties. The question, and the answer, allow both people to empathise with a reality they may not previously have been aware of and therefore actively listening to your teams not only offers you great business benefit, but it inspires and motivates your team as well. In the end, both the giving and the taking of perspectives shines a bright light on issues and opportunities that may be going on in the organisation that were otherwise unheard.

In my own team my favourite way to really encourage this type of **power neutral communication** is to deeply consider using the term "why?" with my team members. For a moment, imagine a situation when a team member approaches you to confirm that they can unfortunately no longer make an important deadline that they had previously committed to you, what would your natural response to that person be?

I would hasten to guess that your instinctive reply would be *"why not?"*

The challenge with this is that it is an innately accusatory reply and it therefore creates an inherently defensive response. People have been programmed over many years to subliminally fear this question, from more senior team members (or from their parents and teachers in childhood!), and it therefore has an unconsciously guarding or protective impact on how they reply.

Next time this occurs, consider changing your response to the words *"what's stopping you?"* You will likely find that the person pauses before launching into a response, you may see their eyes move up or down as they consciously deepen their response and consider the answer more holistically, before answering with far more insight and context than their instinctive quick-fire answer would have revealed. It is really worth giving it a try as it can be an incredibly powerful way to actively

If you are busy thinking about a response when the other person is speaking, you are not listening.

encourage response and to show that you are deeply interested and listening to the person. And after all, what's stopping you?

CLIENT UNDERSTANDING AND LISTENING FOR SUCCESS

Across industries we talk about 'clients' as these foreign and external entities; people we share business with who are somehow distant and not quite like us. It's so strange when you think about it because in nearly every occasion the 'client' has chosen the organisation. They have chosen to work with us and yet we build these subconscious gaping divides between 'us and them.'

There is a deep need for us to train our teams in improving and building client relationships via memorising the skills needed for empathic listening and understanding. Conscious communication in building relationship with clients can lead to far more fruitful and profitable relationships and yet we so infrequently train these skills. Empathic listening, or active listening is easily incorporated into our development programs and whilst it takes some time to master, once it becomes the norm it is a truly powerful skillset at all levels of an organisation.

When client relationships are working well, clients are likely to talk about their most preferred partners as "*listening well*" or "*always understanding what we need*". In any industry there are likely to be hundreds of suppliers that can deliver what the client needs, on time and within budget, but it takes special teams to be able to really hear what the client's problem is and what they are hoping to solve. The work that works, and the work that wins loyalty, not only shows deep understanding of its audience but also represents the depth of the client relationship and trust. Industry-leading work doesn't ever happen without immense amounts of energy spent on the relationship with the client. Of course, there are a host of obvious client-pleasing leadership tactics, but it is the genuine caring that really takes a relationship through a tough or longstanding period. As the world recovered from the COVID-19 pandemic in 2020, there was much discussion about a global recession and a socioeconomic impact over the following 12 to 24 months. It was the client relationships built on something other than delivery alone that weathered those times. **The goodwill and loyalty of deep connectivity may never have been more important or valuable.**

LISTENING IS NOT ALL ABOUT OUR EARS

Deep relationship building takes time, but in the short term a heightened awareness of nonverbal communication, even from clients you don't know well, can significantly improve your ability to listen, and deliver on their needs, more effectively. We have all heard that up to 80 percent of communication is nonverbal, but do we ever actually teach or train our teams how to leverage this? These are skills that have been honed by a blend of evolution, social experience, and parental guidance, so most of us do have them, but so often we leave the use of them to chance. The robust empathetic influence of nonverbal communication and listening is potentially the most underused, yet simple, set of tools available to us.

Empathetic listening is not only about the transfer of words and stories but body language, tone, eye contact, and even the sense of touch. Whether you are an advertising agency working with a client or a corporate business managing global stakeholders, the ability to empathise with your audience to foster better understanding and connection can be significantly improved without saying a word. Let's consider a typical situation in a client and partner relationship.

I will use an advertising agency and client relationship as an example, but the relevance is wide enough to impact any project.

It's a Thursday and the client comes to an advertising agency's office to give them a creative project brief. The briefing goes well, the PowerPoint is slick, and the client is a potent mix of anxious and excited. When the session is complete, the client leaves with a spring in their step and the creative team begins to solve the client brief. The client thinks the agency understood their request and the agency assumes they heard what the client asked for.

Here is the challenge, though. Although the agency team were functionally listening to what the client was saying, they had missed a whole host of the things that were *unsaid*. They missed the part when his tone of voice became significantly more tense, signalling he was most concerned about this area. They missed the part when he crossed his arms and leant back in response to their suggestions, showing that he was absolutely not happy with their direction. They were too busy daydreaming about potential creative solutions to notice when his eyes darted off to the corridor outside and his attention was lost. The agency team had absorbed the *information* but they had totally missed the insight the client had been communicating. The agency partner goes on to complete the work they think perfectly answers the client brief and they are looking forward to sharing it. Alas, the presentation of that work a few weeks later doesn't go to plan. The client is infuriated and frustrated that the agency didn't hear what he originally thought he had 'said'. He feels he had made it very clear, whereas the audience clearly heard something else entirely. The whole room falls into an awkward energy and the process of re-briefing begins.

It wasn't that the team wasn't listening to their client but that there was a lack of active listening in that initial meeting. The agency team were listening for their own output (i.e. what do I need to deliver?), and meanwhile they were ignoring the most important part, which was the input, the context of the speaker, the real needs or desires that the client was hoping they would pick up on. By listening for the output instead of the input, the listener entirely misses the unspoken pressure points;

the part when the client mentions that their boss had asked for some killer detail, or the area that made the client actively uncomfortable.

In the next meeting you attend, watch the speaker's body language and tone of voice. Watch for when they squirm in their chair, bite their lip, dart their eyes away from you, or speak a little faster. Sit in their shoes as they speak, activate your empathetic radar and you will instinctively know when to ask questions or intervene, and where to empathise with the challenge. It is a critical and conscientious skill to be able to know when to stop talking or change tack, to be able to watch the room and understand when to show understanding and agreement, and when to encourage more sharing. The more you do this the better you will get at it, and if you focus on the audience more than the content you will find you gain double the insight out of every meeting. If you accept that the briefing or meeting is the client's best job in the given time (for whatever reason) and make the commitment regardless to gain more than written words and functional requests, a weak brief or meeting need never result in bad work. No client wants their partner to go wrong; it costs them too much in time, money, or reputation so assume positive intention always. There is no deep secret here. **Listening and caring about how the room of people feel is the simplest way to improve business success and relationship building.**

LISTENING YOUR WAY TO SUCCESS

Some years ago, I had a particularly challenging client leader who often struggled to make himself understood by my, or indeed their own, team. I can't count the number of meetings that the client would brief people on something, only to find out the team hadn't understood what he actually wanted. The miscommunication created havoc on both sides of the partnership and over a year passed without it improving. The key to solving this problem was to acutely observe the client's nonverbal communication. I would watch him and take note of the questions that he found most frustrating to answer, and that would speak volumes. I would hear him briefly mention a stakeholder request but watch his entire body tense as he said it, so while everyone else in the room ignored it as a mere passing statement, I noted that this was actually what had been keeping him up at night. By removing the fear, status, or barriers between you and the client, you can approach the meeting simply as two humans connecting on an issue. Even if this doesn't come naturally to you at first, it can be learned with the commitment to doing so.

Consider your own ability to use empathy in your next big meeting. When your key client turns up to a meeting and confirms that a whole host of conversations have been going on over the weekend and their boss has subsequently changed the brief they gave you the week before, take heed before responding. **Pause**. Your instinct might be to give a straightforward response (and an inward sigh of exasperation), asking for details of the amended brief and new timeline, accepting facts as facts and not considering the emotional toll this may have also had on the client. An empathetic listener, however, might respond differently. Their instinctive response might be "*Your boss changed his mind, why? What happened this weekend? How do you feel about it?*" What is pretty critical is that you remove the word 'I' from these sentences. Being empathetic means putting yourself in their shoes—this is about their opinions, not yours. Listen without judgement and without impacting the outcome. I have found that three of the most powerful words in these scenarios are *"tell me more"*. They are open words that encourage communication and sharing. Whilst they are overt in their request they are inquisitive enough to show natural interest to spark more conversation and details. The intention is to obtain understanding and to sincerely identify, and respond to, the emotions or context of the other person (and their boss), and not to simply respond to the changing facts. You will garner far more intel and insight as to what the situation is and how the client is really hoping you can solve it.

In my experience, clients tend to know what they want, but it is in the extracting of this information that the listener can surpass all expectations by accurately responding. I once heard empathetic listening described as a "*butter knife inserted parallel to a stream of water*", which I love. It assumes the ability to inject yourself into someone's monologue without interfering at all. It's the perfect analogy. Empathetic relationships are based on the ability to see and hear your client's context and to open them up as an ally, and when things go really well, a friend. The ability to do this and then to use thoughtful, open-ended questions to invite deeper details or consideration allow your client to open up and be honest about the full picture. Once this connectivity is built and someone truly trusts that you are interested, that you care and that you will really listen to them, the relationship is much more firmly embedded for long-term success. It doesn't matter what level you are or what job title you have, once a client feels that you hear them, it is just human nature to share more openly. Essentially, all of us want someone to listen to us a little more intently. It's human nature.

IT'S ALL IN YOUR EYES. OR IS IT?

We have established that listening isn't something you do only with your ears, and eye contact is arguably one of the most underrated 'listening' tools that we have. People often say that eyes are the window to the soul, and I agree. Not only does eye contact break down barriers but it also tells you something. Begin noticing how many people avoid any level of held gaze in meetings, conversations, and conferences and how many people retreat to their cell phone screen in order to not have to face the eyes of someone else directly. People are uncomfortable with eye contact and yet it is the most integral and deeply human connection point that we have.

A couple of years ago, I was in a very heavy procurement negotiation for a large contract that I knew would significantly change my team's ability to succeed in the year ahead. Not only was I nervous, I also had a sense that we were somehow on the back foot. The negotiator was a very severe Russian- trained financial expert. She was straight faced, emotionally extremely distant, and well versed in how to make supplier teams feel as powerless as possible in this final negotiation stage. What I noticed early on was that she had obviously been told to avoid eye contact. It is common knowledge that eye contact significantly builds relationships, but not many of us think much about the fact that the opposite is also true, and that avoiding eye contact can aid a person when you actively want to create a sense of distance and non-relationship. Top negotiators have this mastered and therefore in these particular negotiations, my attempts to try and change this dynamic took an incredible commitment and energy. It was exhausting to continually try to catch and hold her gaze and she was extremely set on not making this any easier for me! I didn't give up, though, and little by little, as I won over the eyes of the procurement lead, the conversation direction and tone began to change. Managing to capture our shared humanity was more powerful, and more natural, than either of our training programmes in 'successful negotiation' had been. Once we could look at each other directly, the conversation became far more human and far less stilted and script-following. This was important to me because I wanted her to understand my intentions and to therefore sign the agreement because she trusted me that it was accurate and fair. I believed that it truly represented a reflection of the support and service her organisation needed to succeed and I wanted her to know the truth of that intention. In the end she did. The eye contact won, and to my relief, she signed.

A few weeks later she greeted me with two kisses in reception and my heart skipped as I internally celebrated an extremely long journey from icy corporate management to an honest human connection as two specialists in our own fields. I really enjoyed our meetings and she told me that day that our negotiations were the only ones she looked forward to. We won more than a fee approval in that process; we won an ally in a key department in the client's business.

MOVING YOUR BODY TO MOVE ON CONVERSATIONS

However important eye contact is, the rest of your body language also acts as a key empathetic signal for those you work with. Maintaining eye contact but with a stiff back, crossed arms, severe mouth, and a raised chin will do you no favours at all. Body language is so much more than just connected eyes.

You may find that you have to concentrate far harder on your arms than you do your eyes; it is very easy to fall back into crossing your arms and closing off your body while looking directly at someone and sharing a greeting. Whether your client or audience could tell you overtly that you are doing it is up for debate, but for sure subconsciously they are reading it and responding accordingly. Far from being empathetically connected, your arms are creating distance, and perhaps disagreement or disrespect without you ever consciously realising it. To truly listen, you need your entire body to listen, not just your ears or your eyes by being open to receiving the other person's message. Evolution has taught all of us how to instinctively respond more positively to an open versus a closed audience. You will find that across all of society, if you physically lean toward or turn toward those you are talking to, the entire discussion and energy changes. The person you are talking to will likely lean in as well and they will mirror your actions and connectivity. The act of doing so is known as mirroring and I will unpack it a little further at the end of this chapter. It is an extremely powerful skill to finesse. Sometimes, depending on the context or audience, it might take some time, but I have never seen an occasion when it doesn't happen eventually. It's natural. We have evolved to reciprocate empathetic connection and using your body to do so is the most basic of forms. It is the core of nonverbal cultural signage that you are connected to the other person, that you are invested and attempting to be worthy of their words and input. What I find is that for every moment you invest into proving you are interested and present, and therefore worthy of their sharing, the more likely the other person is to give you their ears and their minds. Presence unto itself is very impactful and therefore the quality and the scope of the content improves the more present, and therefore connected, you become. Proving presence is something that equally takes conscious effort (until it becomes your natural state) and involves a mix of body language, tone, and focus. For me personally, I ensure I don't ever allow myself to worry about the other 237 things on my to-do list, nor do I concern myself with what will happen as the clock hits fifty-nine minutes past the hour and the plans for the next meeting commence. It is only by really being in this meeting, for the whole thing including the final sixty seconds, that you can get all the value that you set out to achieve or receive. When the clock does reach the hour and you apologise to the person but mention you need to leave, they tend not to mind one bit because they feel that you gave them everything you had in the time you shared. You were 100 percent present for them and for the duration of that meeting. This carries its weight in gold in our ever distracted and technologically interrupted age.

The drawback to this is that it can be pretty exhausting! By the end of the day and the completion of twelve or fifteen meetings or engagements, where you have fully leant in to every person you met with (including the engagement with the barista at the coffee shop and the taxi driver you flew between meetings with), you are tired. This is one of the shadows that an empathetic leader may carry. The balance however is that by the end of that day not only have you impacted the micro moments of everyone you met but you have also gained 100 percent of the value you went into all those meeting or engagements to offer, so the exhaustion becomes absolutely worth it.

LOOKING IN THE MIRROR

The final part of empathetic client relationship building is based on mirroring, which is the ability to match or reflect the actions of another. It is often the most charismatic and genuine business people that have this mastered, and as a technique for building rapport it's a strong contender for our leading relationship-building superpower.

Have you ever noticed that the more you match your own expressions to the person you are listening to or engaging with, the more they tend to offer or respond? Imagine a couple in a bar talking animatedly about a plan or a deal. They are leaning in and are almost hunched over as they discuss a new project in detail. Their body language is as engrossed with the other person as the content of their conversation is, and the more they share, the closer they physically lean in. Their shared body language and the cohesive spoken language are in sync.

It may not be something you do naturally, all the time, but a conscious commitment to doing so may begin to create far deeper and more open conversations. Matching another's style and approach is a natural sign of respect that evolution has taught us to instinctively respond to. It shows your counterpart that you understand them.[xcii]

Mirroring has a wide set of capabilities. It can extend from the basics of body language (they lean in, so do you, they cross their arms, so do you) to tone of voice, speed of the conversation and even the approach to the conversation by matching, for example, a results orientated or more conversational style with similar response style. Often you can guide the person you are meeting with to become more relaxed or engaged by honing the ability to reflect them. The better the mirroring the more neutral ground is created and the physical response becomes an equaliser. It almost instantly makes people subconsciously soften and open up their behaviour and attitude towards you.

If you enter a meeting, for example, where the energy is tense and the speaker is extremely formal, being too relaxed or gregarious at the outset will create distance between you. By reflecting and mimicking similar environmental and social cues, however, you are showing the most basic form of empathy and respect for their context. When you deliberately, but not overtly, start to match the pace, tone, gestures and focus of your audience, both networking and negotiating are heightened. (Of course, the balance is not to overly copy someone's actions and behaviour—this might become very awkward—but to naturally create common ground and receptivity.)

The best part of the mirroring techniques? Smiling.

Have you ever noticed that smiling itself is contagious?! Smiling might just be the most influential asset in your relationship building toolkit.

"IF SPEAKING IS SILVER, THEN LISTENING IS GOLD."

TURKISH PROVERB

I don't think we should ever underestimate smiling in the working world. It is a fundamentally neutralising, evolutionary, and natural response for all human beings and the more we smile the more we thrive. We are tuned to naturally and openly respond to a smile by smiling back because smiling creates a symbiotic relationship. Put simply, it makes both people feel better, more connected, more relaxed and less stressed. To that end, ask yourself the question: **Was there ever a working relationship, negotiation or conversation that wasn't enhanced by both parties feeling in tune, at peace and connected with each other?**

Our mirror neurons in our brains stimulate our own smiling when we see someone smile and that instantly creates a sensorial reward. We feel better. Just try to frown whilst looking at someone with a beaming wide smile; it really is almost impossible! This is, in part, because we evolved knowing that it is rewarding to be smiled at. It was Louis Armstrong who confirmed to us, in arguably his most famous song, that when we smile the whole world smiles with us. Our facial muscles will naturally mirror those of another as a subconscious ability that we practise all the way from tiny infant life. We are tuned to the fact that when a baby smiles at us, we respond with a wide and celebratory smile back; we are engraining the behaviour from that very first happy moment.

Given smiling produces happy hormones (dopamine, serotonin, and endorphins) it bears true and valid that we could do worse than to smile a little more often when trying to transform business relationships. Whilst a smile often follows something joyful or funny, smiling unto itself makes us feel more joy. Stress goes down, empathy goes up, and the world (of business) becomes a happier, more connected place. It's not only infectious, it's powerfully community and connectivity building.

The rallying cry of this chapter is to **command less and listen more**. Lean in more, mirror more, be more connected. Not just with your ears but with your entire being. Honing your ability to listen to your people, to really hear them, and to respond to them effectively will create monumental steps toward deeper connectivity and kinship with those around you. It will help you empathise mutually as well as improve relationships, build bridges, and drive shared business interest upward. Begin by bringing consciousness to using these skills with your team and clients, and then continue to do that until you find you don't have to think about it anymore. Fortunately, instinctively you already know how to do much of this so I am sure you will be thrilled how easily you can integrate this into your team.

As you build a more empathetic listening culture you will start to notice that your team is more deeply connected. If you do nothing else in the weeks ahead, give some of these techniques a go. **After all, what's stopping you?**

Chapter 18

THE ART OF CONNECTING WITH CONSUMERS

A study by Steelcase and Microsoft reports that 77 percent of people believe creativity is a key skill for any twenty-first- century role, yet according to Forrester, 61 percent of leaders say they don't currently believe their company is creative enough.[xciii] Beyond this, recent data from Orlando Wood's book, *Lemon,* states that we have a "crisis in creativity" and that we have seen an ongoing and drastic decline in creative effectiveness in the years between 2008 and 2018.[xciv] Is it possible that our empathy deficit is also killing our creativity?

Creativity is a differentiator, a change maker, a pace driver, and is so often at the core of all valuable transformation. **It is the magic that takes good ideas to truly resonant and connected movements—movements of mindsets, movements of behaviour, and movements of goods and sales.** It is the kinesiology of the corporate world, stirring us and shifting our opinions, and it is a shared currency for connectivity. At its core, the best of creativity and innovation is born from empathetic understanding. How else would we be able to impact humanity so profoundly?

Those who create stories, poetry, art, music, and yes, advertising, understand something about you that perhaps even you didn't even know. They see you, they hear you, they watch you in the most observant of ways. They paint a picture for you to dive into, a belief that you want to be part of or a feeling you want to keep forever. They tap into society, into humanity, and into reality. **They may sell stories but empathy is their currency.** When Dr Helen Riess talks about empathetic "capacity" she refers to it as "*a human capacity consisting of several different facets that work together to enable us to be moved by the plights and emotions of others*".[xcv] Now surely, put in another context, that is the best description of the role of creative marketing that we have ever heard?

Why?

Because the roots of all expressionism, which sees artists look inward to channel their ability to reflect society and connect with people, are grounded by empathy. At its simplest, all forms of art are bedded in the ability to honestly reflect the voice of some, to an audience of others, in a way that allows the audience, by way of imagination, to project themselves into another's story.

To empathise is to imagine, to empathise is to understand, and to empathise is to share.

The commercial art of business is no different. Throughout history we have been projecting the stories of others into a form of output that provokes behavioural change, and ideally a sale. Movies, music videos, and the top viral content, are all formats that share the same thing: a story about humanity that we want to hear. A story that stirs or provokes us. A story that makes us happy, sad, fearful, or angry. A story that allows us to empathise with each other, with a stranger, or even with ourselves! Empathy is at the core of every skill the creative and entertainment industries rely on to connect with their audience to make them feel something.

It follows therefore that some of the best empathetic influencers on the planet are actors. Actors spend their days empathising with a character and using that ability to make a blockbuster film, or hot new Netflix series, into a hook that people will watch for hours at a time, all in a world that claims to have an issue with diminishing attention spans. The reality is that we humans don't have an issue with our attention, we have an issue with what we place our attention on. People like content that connects with them or reminds them of something resonant or rewarding. They enjoy pieces of work that mean something, that are emotive and engaging, that make the time spent watching insignificant against the emotional gains they take away. People respond to stories that have humans, people like them, people they know or want to know, reflected at the core.

Documentary film producer Tabitha Jackson framed this beautifully when she said: *"There are incredibly important stories to be told and injustices to be highlighted. A documentary camera is a kind of empathy machine. It can put you in someone else's shoes."* [xcvi] In some ways it is artists and not philosophers who truly keep we humans complicit in the world we share, whether that is art on a wall, an experiential installation, a book, or even a new office design. It is the special ability to unite as people within a

"MAKING ART ASSUMES EMPATHY. MAKING ART IS THE ACT OF SHARING. IT IS BY DEFINITION AN INVITATION TO OTHERS TO LEAVE THEIR ISOLATION AND MEET OTHERS ON THE SAME ROAD. AN ARTIST WITHOUT EMPATHY IS A SOCIOPATH."

STEVEN HOMES, ARTIST

shared space or context. There is a Portuguese proverb, *"O artista e a voz do povo"* that translates as "artists are the voice of the people". Without empathy, all these mediums become technical, functional deliverables with very little ability to do anything but creating something to look at. I fear that much of our marketing today falls into this trap.

THE POWER OF DEEPLY UNDERSTANDING

Any marketer or strategist who has ever set success principles early in a project knows that understanding your audience is foundational for business results. Whether we are innovating a product, creating a new pricing strategy, or launching a new marketing campaign, it is insight into our audience that assures us the work will work. **Empathy is the secret path to all deeply resonant and powerful insights**, and it is a skill that the best communicators and content creators around the world instinctively deliver in every project. Empathetic understanding leads to that ever sought after 'aha' moment that a strategist has when they realise they have uncovered a truly powerful human emotion. It is what hundreds of thousands of marketers subconsciously work toward every day. After all, provoking action requires a deeply accurate and honest human relevance. We humans know what authentic looks like; we know 'real life' when we see it. It is our ability to see ourselves or the things we care about or know by memory structure, that gives creativity its unending power.

What all great artists instinctively know is that if we become too self-involved and remove human connection from the work, it stops working. The work becomes isolating and disconnecting and the medium stops encouraging people to lean in and listen. We are talking to ourselves.

Fundamentally, empathetic communication is the communication that connects a brand or business with its audience. It unifies them. In order to move people to action we have to share stories, and it is the empathy in the storytelling that makes those stories meaningful enough to stimulate experiences that encourage action and growth. Empathetic insight and its influence, within the creative ideas it sparks, is vital to creating marketing and innovation ideas that reflect the world we live in, love in, and dream about.

THE FLEXIBILITY OF CREATIVITY

Never have I entered a room with any client specialism, from marketing to finance to business operations, **where creativity hasn't significantly improved the outcome**. Human beings are inspired incrementally by creative stimulus. You can see it from the very moment babies begin to see the world. It is colour, art, music, and eclectic environments that attract the highest response. We are naturally drawn to things that drive our imagination, revelation, and artistry. It is only as we grow that we think our jobs are too serious or 'corporate' to incorporate something as 'fickle' or open to interpretation as creativity. From million-dollar renewals of intranet service systems, legal services, or aircraft ground handling equipment, there is nothing that creativity can't help trade.

As the level of sophistication and complexity in a business increases, and when every decision has a wide- reaching organisational impact, the decision to buy into, sign, or agree to a proposal is arguably more complex and deeper than on any other occasion. When a CTO is choosing whether to implement a cloud-based storage solution for a multimillion-dollar business, they know that it is not solely for the good of the company, which may be their main goal, but also that they are being judged personally for the choice they make. If they don't make the right decision, they run the risk of being fired by someone who will. The decision to purchase has both a corporate lens and a personal lens complexly blurred together. The opportunity to connect with the personal investment in the decision making is much higher when there is empathy in understanding the buyer's reality alongside the creativity to package it in a consumable way. The need to capture thought at a more intuitive and human level can be the difference between that decision maker saying "yes" or "no" when comparing otherwise similar offerings.

Creativity is as much a feeling as it is thinking; it is the most flexible form of message propagation and benefit communication that we have. It travels literally and laterally and evokes an openness to consider, reconsider, and in the best of times, repurchase. In the business world, creativity plays a critical role across the value chain. When you practise more creativity in your business environments you will notice that people are more open and more engaged with nearly everything you present to them. Creativity creates connectivity, and connectivity sells.

MARKETING EMPATHY

In recent years, Forrester Consulting discovered that 65 percent of marketers struggle to employ emotional marketing as they turn to automation to improve customer engagement. With all the 'buttons' we have available to us, to slice, dice, and divide data and mass communications, how have we come to lose the empathy button?

The more we automate away from our human instincts, the harder it is to get people to trust us, yet we know that trust drives revenue. Fundamentally, we will never be able to automate trust. Trust is something created, crafted, and cared for. Although robots and augmented reality beings may help us with efficiency, speed, and process, they cannot compete on our innate human ability to look someone in the eye and promise them something. At least, not yet!

You can find hundreds of examples of people talking about how the marketing world needs to entirely reconstruct around the technical, 'data-led' age, but I don't subscribe to this rhetoric as a standalone argument. We are seeing a decrease in marketing effectiveness and an increase in functional, benefit-led communications, and the equation connecting them is pretty clear. The less emotive and human our marketing becomes, the less it works. Nothing creatively world-changing ever came out of a perfectly formatted data set. **Creativity is born from the heart, from a gut feel, an intuitive response, or a moment of madness but never a spreadsheet.**

We have more technology to connect with consumers than ever before and more data to leverage an understanding of what people want, yet the systematic dehumanisation by corporate agendas, procurement processes, and over-analysis has damaged our ability to connect. Artificial intelligence and chatbots can move us toward the promise of personalised marketing, and yet so often the technology ends up feeling inauthentic and 'cold'. As marketers, it is our intuition and integrity in empathising with the real and honest problems that will allow us to really make an impact and turn a mundane click into a loyal client over time. **Empathy is our data set.**

The best of stories can *only* be told if the writer has a true understanding of those they are writing about, and to gain this insight they will always need to be able to understand society around them. Satya Nadella states: *"Our core business is connected with the customers' needs and we will not be able to satisfy them if we don't have a deep sense of empathy."*

Fundamentally, marketing was never meant to be something you do 'to' people but something you do 'with' people. A two-way connection that offers value on both sides. As humans we like to be heard and to be noticed, and when we feel we are, we act positively toward the person, brand, or entity that is doing so. This is the secret to all the best marketing campaigns.

EMPATHY IN UNLIKELY PLACES

When you think of debt collecting, what comes to mind? Aggression? Tension? Urgency? Certainly, I suspect, not empathy.

You could be excused for thinking this is the last place empathy has a role, but then you have probably never heard of a company called CFS2 in the USA. CFS2 is a debt collection agency that doesn't hire debt collectors. At CFS2, their business strategy is to hire experienced customer services employees who can coach and talk people through their debt issues. Many years ago, the organisation recognised that the reality is that most people being chased by debt collectors can't pay (which is pretty obvious when you think about it!), and therefore the fear tactics used industry wide to try and force payment were flawed. Fundamentally, the CFS2 team identified an empathy gap. They therefore decided to mentor and support indebted people into getting jobs, upskilling their talent, joining resume workshops, or looking at their lifestyle to improve their financial planning. Their strategy was to increase the chances of their 'clients' paying back their debt by driving their clients' financial and personal wellbeing. In the business world, **what is measured, manifests**. The CFS2 employees are measured and rewarded not by how much money they collect. but by how many free financial support services they provide. The results of this entirely innovative and human approach to the industry show that the company was 200 percent more profitable than their competition and the founder was nominated for a Nobel Peace Prize.[xcix] Humanity reflected by business innovation, and profit levels that justify every decision the brand made to empathise with versus chastise those in debt.

Thanks to the industry patterns of the last three decades, a generation of marketing leaders before us allowed empathy to be viewed as unquantifiable in the industry. These leaders hid from it and erred toward functional benefit-led communication that is now commonplace. For many marketers, functional communications are less scary, less subjective, and far easier to input onto a spreadsheet—but they are also far less relatable, effective, or relevant to any audience member anywhere! Over time this has led to a belief that people will buy more if you link products to their aspirations instead of actually being interested in their realities. Many brands and marketers have become ego- or organisation-centric, thinking more about what the brand (or marketing team!) wants than what the consumer wants. Having spent a career sitting through in- depth research debriefs, I know this to be true. By the time the research has been completed, at great expense, it becomes the marketer's choice what to listen to and what not to, and when large amounts of time and money are at play, the discounting of macro relevance can often be easily sacrificed for speed to market. The lack of understanding of their audience screams inauthenticity but no one seems to care.

In the years that drove the Empathy Gap into society and corporate life, the advertising and marketing industry simultaneously distanced themselves from the humanity of the buyers they should have valued. As conspicuous consumption continued to rise, and people really did create a sense of self based on the products they bought, those behind the ads turned off their emotional intelligence. As I write, there is a multimillion-dollar advertising campaign live locally for a washing powder. It is a brand refresh and I am sure it will do wonders for awareness because you can't miss it, it's everywhere. I am a consumer of the brand, but every time I see the ads all I want to do is ask "who signed it off?" The campaign shows people of all kinds animatedly and enthusiastically throwing washing tabs into empty (yes, empty!) washing machines from all types of angles and homes. It attempts to make doing the laundry seem like an altogether fun and exciting activity, to convince us to swap from washing powder to washing tabs. I just cannot imagine the meeting where this work was presented and loved. At what stage did the team think that people's home lives reflect, or want to reflect, this even remotely? When did the research team (if there was one) agree that the human insight underpinning this work had even a strain of semblance to humanity? Have you ever met anyone who wishes the washing was more fun? Quicker, more effective, less hard work, maybe. But entertaining? Doubtful. I also suspect it is unlikely that you can remember the last time you popped home thinking *gosh I can't wait to throw that washing tab into my washing machine" or, if I am being less cynical, "gosh I am just so glad that washing powder brand has shown me a more fun way to fill the machine. I must swap to that brand immediately."*

I don't mean to bash the work, honestly, I don't, but if we are talking about empathetic gaps between marketers and people, here we have one. The marketing is just so far from reality, from real life, that no wonder the industry is not trusted. Perhaps it worked well for the brand, the media money alone will have driven up recall and familiarity

TO EMPATHISE =
TO EMPATHISE =
TO EMPATHISE =

IMAGINE. UNDERSTAND. SHARE.

and maybe that's all that matters? But, when we have the opportunity to tell a story that reflects human behaviour, that is designed with people in mind and can reach millions of people, why wouldn't you grab that with both hands? You could be making a difference! A real life, home-life, human difference. A missed opportunity, a gap in empathy, and a marketing trend we see far too much of.

THE FIVE WHYS TO EMPATHETIC UNDER-STANDING

In Bangkok many years ago, a colleague taught me a really simple tool to help uncover insights that can help us avoid work that is detached from its audience. It is called 'The Five Whys'.

I absolutely love it as a tool for driving empathy into business solutions because it genuinely works. It's amazingly simple and yet deeply astute, and it works like this...

Drum roll...

You ask "why" five times.
That's it.

Ask "why" five times to any given question, action, behaviour, assumption, or pattern and then watch what that does to your depth of connection to and understanding of the audience.

Here's an example:

1. You go into a meeting and the client says, *"We need to launch this premium water brand from France to high net worth Arab women who currently don't buy our water"*, and the first thing you ask is *"why?"*

2. Now the marketer will initially give you an answer about market penetration or market share growth, or perhaps they will jump to why they think these Arab women aren't buying the brand, but here's the thing, it's rehearsed. Not in a bad way but they know the answer as top of mind, they were told it or taught it by their

boss or wider organisation, or it's simply common knowledge to date. Either way it's functional and useful but not particularly valuable beyond that. So you listen intently and then, here is your invitation to ask '*why*' again.

3. This time the 'why' is no longer with regard to the first question, but the first answer, so you will find the client digs deeper into their answer without even realising they are doing it. Suddenly their simple answer that Arab women aren't buying their brand because it's more expensive may get unpacked further when they mention that actually there is a barrier in the belief that water from Europe is any more pure or mineral rich than the cheaper water they are already buying, or that the local market likes to support local brands, or that their current imported water already holds their hearts. This starts to unpack a consumer belief, a real barrier, or an inflection point.

4. By the time you ask the third 'why' you will find your client is either making some assumptions of their own (which in themselves will be valuable because they are bound to be based on valuable intel or instinct) or they are asking a few questions of their own. Whichever is the case, they are engaged and 'awake' to their own brief and challenge in a far deeper way. The rationale behind the consumer barrier or belief starts to fill up with human behaviour and nuances, and even a few assumptions. All of which make for great creativity 'fodder'.

5. I won't go into the next two 'whys', but you get the idea. With every 'why' you unpack a deeper understanding of the previous answer to the 'why' before. Give it a try yourself. Ask a friend or family member about the takeout food they choose, or the rationale behind your daughter's request to upgrade her laptop and you will begin to see how the tool works. Wherever you apply The Five Whys you will find you embark on the most phenomenal journey into deeper empathetic relevance and

understanding of what people really want, or how they feel. I have never met anyone that isn't hooked on it once they give it a go.

There is a scene in *The Good Wife* (a longstanding successful US legal drama that swallowed up many hours of my life before I started writing a book!) where the protagonist gets promoted to partner in her law firm. From that moment on she begins receiving direct mail to her desk full of offers for yachts, private villas, and glamorous holiday destinations that she has zero interest in. It's as if a new job title has miraculously transformed her overnight into a new person with a new set of habits and lifestyle choices. It's a perfect example of what happens to us as consumers every day. Brands bundle us into mundane groups based our sex, race, employment, or shopper data, and approach us with solutions they think we might want. They rarely ask us beforehand and they infrequently check in afterward. We feel they don't care about us and by all accounts we are not far wrong. The data the brand uses to group us is based on an algorithm for our behaviour, style, or context, and the importance of our emotion or opinion is downplayed if not entirely bypassed. To further a contentious issue, the data collection process rarely asks us whether the data set was a relevant or authentic reflection of us in the first place. Just because I searched for red shoes to

"THE SOURCE OF INNOVATION IS YOUR ABILITY TO GRASP THE UNMET, UNARTICULATED NEEDS OF CUSTOMERS. IT COMES FROM EMPATHY."

SATYA NADELLA, CEO MICROSOFT

match my best friend's wedding once last summer, does not make me a red shoe shopper. The data never asked me why I searched, and for sure I didn't ask them to help me fill my cupboard with any more of those grudge wedding purchases.

By no means am I against data or the leverage of big data sets. The evolution of data has huge power to help marketers adopt and build on behavioural patterns, but without the humanity, humility, and empathy to analyse it, the data remains digits. As AI improves our analytical ability at scale, the 'machines' will get ever better at automating our general understanding of our audiences, but machines without the masterful eye of people will always open up the risk of stereotyping and exclusion. AI reduces our ability to find the story in the pattern and identify the often-irrational habits of real people; just because 85 percent of a particular set of postcode data tells the story of an underprivileged neighbourhood with low educational standards, does not mean the next Elon Musk was not born there. Equally, just because your medical data looks to predict high propensity to a heart attack doesn't mean it is necessarily going to happen 'to you'.

As data becomes more ubiquitous, the incorporation of empathy will critically humanise and protect our organisations, and our marketing, from potential multimillion-dollar failures. Empathy adds human *values* and not just the *value* of the data to our understanding and activation of reflecting the relationship we want to build with that audience. None of this is to say that data doesn't drive our understanding of consumer habits and behaviour, but simply that we need to recognise that much decision making is emotional and heavily influenced by lifelong attitudes and legacy or cultural beliefs, which a data set cannot be expected to reflect. It is in the softening of the edges

---

Our personal assumptions drown out our ability to empathise, and it's happening so subconsciously we often don't even realise we are doing it.

---

of the data that we ultimately drive resonance. The empathetic leverage of data enables organisations today to be simultaneously left and right brained, fusing data optimisation with human passion for grounded yet magical connections.

The brands and businesses that tell stories that demonstrate their respect and empathy for their audience make money. It's that simple. Our ability to see the world from the perspective of others is one of the most crucial differentiators in the global marketplace today.

Creativity is not for the faint hearted, it is for the full hearted, and that is why empathy so accurately and powerfully collides within the creative industries. Whether it is due to the increasing fear culture across organisations, a new generation of marketers who are so hooked on digital data they have lost their ability to 'feel', or timelines that squash every project into an ever downward race against time, we are seeing brands frequently miss this deeper connection. The Empathy Advantage can be as powerful an approach to external brand building and communication strategy as it can be internally. **By seeing and evaluating our brands as living, changing, and feeling entities, we can reassess how to create communications that truly reflect what they can offer or fulfil.**

Brands today are too often seen as individual, standalone entities, but in truth they are a collation of authentic human stories. We need to sell them that way.

STOP

Chapter 19

STOPPING THE DECLINE BEFORE THE DECLINE STOPS US

The world is changing and the Empathy Deficit that Barack Obama coined nearly fifteen years ago has been silently deepening ever since.[c] We are facing economic, social, and political crises in nearly every corner of our planet, and the impact is that people have been divided as we individually bed down to care for our own, in place of the natural need and ability to empathise with the wider community around us.

As the fourth revolution evolves and we spend more time on a screen than we do sleeping,[ci] virtual connections, shared work and living spaces, and an always-connected cell phone mean that we are closer together than ever before, yet socially we are suffering with the highest levels of loneliness, anxiety, and depression, along with epidemic proportions of burnout. It was estimated by the World Health Organization in 2015 that more than 322 million people have depression and that these cases saw a steep increase of 18.4 percent between 2005 and 2015. The numbers are rising as our people are falling.[cii]

Suicide rates are the highest they have been for half a century and society appears to be less civil, settled, or stable than ever before. Increased stress, extreme independence, and lower perceived security are just some of the reasons behind humanity's modern-day strain. Increased polarisation in political ideologies, the rise of cyberbullying, and the lack of connection between teachers and their students, doctors and their patients, and CEOs and their teams are growing in number and impact daily.

The sad reality is that it doesn't need to be this way.

These are not empathetic gaps caused by a lack of empathetic ability but a lack of motivation or understanding for the social need to do so. A lack of consciousness around the benefit of understanding and connecting with those in the figurative, and literal, villages around us. A lack of caring and compassion for our fellow human beings.

We have reached a point as a global community where the Empathy Deficit is changing our ability to see the perspective of each other at extreme levels. From politicians to doctors, CEOs to activists, so many of us are significantly misunderstanding the powerfully impressive role increased empathy could be having on society, our businesses, and our organisations at large, particularly in a post COVID-19 world, when we will see a need to develop our innate ability to leverage empathetic connection on a far more wide-reaching scale. The lack of doing so threatens our social fabric, our corporations, and the future of generations to come.

There is a small but growing number of individuals who are driving the agenda for this conversation to change, but the volume is far from loud enough. It is time, dear reader.

Today.

Time to reclaim our empathy, humanity's oldest leadership trait, and commit to creating a practice within our businesses and communities that can significantly intervene.

This book is a gesture. It creates the opportunity for comprehending that regenerative leaders are perfectly placed, and critically responsible for, playing a role in protecting and improving our future. From the development of pro- social behaviour, non-judgemental attitudes, and altruistic helping behaviour, to lowering the levels of stress, antisocial behaviour, and bullying, as leaders we are able to create a stronger ability for people to thrive. We have the ripple power to regenerate people as well as regenerate business.

More than any other species on Earth, humans vicariously experience the realities and feelings of others.[ciii] It is our superpower. It is evolution's unkept, and so far often overlooked, secret. Yet for all its beneficial facets, and it's almost inexplicably magical ability to change perspectives and performance, alongside its deep connection to joy, **we are still choosing the self over the social time and again.**

Even with all the research that exists, alongside our own evolutionary history, empathy is still not felt or being leveraged in a resounding number of businesses today. Practising empathetic skills will allow today's leaders to powerfully impact how people work in groups, connect with each other, deliver results, and treat one another in all areas of life. The act of empathetic influence itself creates a positive outcome for both the 'empathiser' and the empathy target in a uniquely reciprocal engagement. It makes us feel good and do good, and it can fundamentally grow our organisations by directly impacting the bottom line as well as the emotional health of those who will lead the change.

"TO ACHIEVE PEACE, JUSTICE AND INCLUSION, IT IS IMPORTANT THAT GOVERNMENTS, CIVIL SOCIETY AND COMMUNITIES WORK TOGETHER TO IMPLEMENT LASTING SOLUTIONS TO REDUCE VIOLENCE, DELIVER JUSTICE AND ENSURE INCLUSIVE PARTICIPATION AT ALL TIMES. FREEDOM TO EXPRESS VIEWS MUST BE GUARANTEED AND PEOPLE MUST BE ABLE TO CONTRIBUTE TO DECISIONS THAT AFFECT THEIR LIVES."

UNITED NATIONS, SUSTAINABLE DEVELOPMENT GOALS

Empathy in the workplace allows us to bring our souls into our roles and thrive as happier humans.

As we have uncovered, there is much research proving that when people can feel the benefits of empathy, they are more open to activating their own empathetic influence, and **empathetic influence influences performance**. Whether via coaching, virtual reality experiences, or empathetic challenges within corporate life, the practice of empathy, and the teaching of the practice, is desperately needed in our workplaces today. We can create a ripple effect if we only commit to doing so. Regenerative leaders need only commit to consciously positioning conscientious culture as a strategic imperative in order to immediately impact the winds of change. We have a chance to slow the pace of the empathetic decline across the world that has been growing for three decades, and it is my hope that *Empathy At Work* will be a part of the elevation of that conversation.

So how do we increase the motivation for change and how do we create a far-reaching practice amongst the leaders of today, and more importantly, the leaders who will take us into the future?

It is time to train. To teach. To elevate the conversation and change the narrative. To start telling the stories of empathetic influence and conscientious Regenerative Leadership more often. And, most importantly, **it's time to practise at large. We need to prove the value of the practice and embed empathy into far more winning scenarios.** It is time to move from simply a value exchange to an exchange of values between our people, our partners, and our stakeholders. Empathy is malleable, so if we can connect empathy to our most senior leaders, we can manifest the change at a speed that resembles progress.

Given science proves that empathy feels good, and that people essentially choose to empathise when given the chance, the barrier we need to leap over is one of beliefs and frequency. [civ] This is deeply heartening because these are barriers that, given time, we can address. Empathy can be taught, depths of data have proven it, but of the many research papers I have read, nearly all point to the requirement of some form of conscious intervention to make the change happen. It is the job of regenerative leaders to provoke that intervention.

The best things in life have never been the easiest things to conquer, and this journey will be no different. The transformation will take immense amounts of grit, patience, and humanity at an always-on scale. It will challenge us and exhaust us, and imbue our already busy leadership roles with additional layers of emotional intelligence. But when you step back and look at the alternative, firstly, we really have no choice, and secondly, we will find great reward, hope, and happiness in our actions. It will further change the way we see the world and our roles, and it will open up relationships and reciprocal success in ways we are missing today. The return on our efforts will alter our future and our outlook. **It will matter.**

Empathetic leadership is not for the faint hearted. It's always-on, it's costly in terms of time, and it can be painfully emotional. It can conflict with your own corporate goals and the navigation of emotional intelligence can be heavy to bear alone. But when all is said and done, it is a choice we absolutely need more leaders to make. For the individuals they influence and the villages they create. For the ripple each and every one of them can have on a far wider subset of humanity than they will ever realise.

My principles are principles of people, but they are not mine alone. The conversation is spreading fast, and although I know few of them personally, I feel deeply motivated by, and connected to, the quality and standing of other leaders leading with a similar message. Barack Obama may have started the conversation, but there are many of the world's leading CEOs, politicians, and academics continuing it. We know we are not born with a fixed amount of empathy; it is an art and a competence we can master and inspire in those around us.[cv]

The only question left to ask is **what role will you take in helping to stop the Empathy Deficit from taking over another decade of humanity's wellbeing?**

Whatever you choose, here's to a positive ripple effect in the years ahead. Here's to a stronger post COVID-19 world where the discussion around empathetic influence can be a beacon of change and of our uniquely human ability to inspire people and more deeply understand them. In hope and in humankind's happiness.

May this book be the beginning of your own conversation and practice of humanity's greatest trait, or if not so bold, may it simply be a reminder that in practising empathy you will always be doing the right thing. For your business, for your team, and for the world.

Because after all, **practice creates permanence.**

“BE THE CHANGE

THAT YOU WISH TO SEE IN THE WORLD."

"Let me
hold the door for you.
I may have
never walked
in your shoes,
but I can see
your soles are worn,
your strength is torn
under the weight of a story
I have never lived before.
Let me hold the door for you.
After all you've walked through,
It's the least I can do."

WITH PERMISSION FROM MORGAN HARPER NICHOLS

ABOUT MIMI

Mimi Nicklin is an internationally bestselling author, the award-winning Founder of the world's widest-reaching organisational empathy platform, Empathy Everywhere, and the top 5-rated podcast host of 'The MiMi YouYou Show'.

She specialises in Listening-Led Leadership and the balance of humanism and capitalism in the workplace. She is an experienced organisational coach, and a well-known thought leader advocating for the global movement to balance humanism and capitalism in our workplaces. She has 60,000 followers on social media and has trained 12,500+ professionals in Fortune 500 organisations, focusing on the future of Empathetic Leadership and Psychological Safety.

@miminicklin

www.linkedin.com/in/miminicklin/

www.miminicklin.com / www/empathyeverywhere.co

REFERENCES AND SOURCES

I **The 2016 Shift Index.** Deloitte. [Online] March 6, 2017. https://www2.deloitte.com/us/en/insights/multimedia/infographics/shift-index.html?icid=dcom_promo_featured|us;en.

II **Morelix, Arnobio**. This Yearlong Study Says Entrepreneurship Is Booming. Here's Why Small Businesses Aren't Feeling It. Inc.com. [Online] April 19, 2019. https://www.inc. com/arnobio-morelix/inc-entrepreneurship-index-2018-q4.html

III **University of Michigan.** Empathy: College students don't have as much as they used to. [Online] May 27, 2010. https://news.umich.edu/empathy-college-students-don-t-have- as-much-as-they-used-to/

IV **Razon, Na'amah & Marsh, Jason**. Empathy on the Decline. Greater Good Magazine. [Online] January 28, 2011

V https://www.theguardian.com/news/2018/jun/04/what-is-depression-and-why-is-it- rising / https://adaa.org/understanding-anxiety/depression

VI **UNHCR. Syria Emergency.** [Online] April 19, 2018. unhcr.org/uk/syria-emergency. html /

VII **Sharman, John**. Coronavirus in numbers as confirmed cases reach 1 million. The Independent. [Online] April 3, 2020

VIII **Northwestern University.** Obama to Graduates: Cultivate Empathy. [Online] June 19, 2016. https://www.northwestern.edu/newscenter/stories/2006/06/barack.html

IX **McLaren, Karla**. Einfühlung and Empathy: What do they mean? [Online] 2013. https:// karlamclaren.com/einfuhlung-and-empathy

X **Ibid.**

XI **Henley, Dede**. Should We Be Happy At Work? Forbes. [Online] April 30, 2018. https://www.forbes.com/sites/dedehenley/2018/04/30/should-we-be-happy-at-work/#14d8027f59ea

XII https://www.azquotes.com/quote/639304

XIII **McChrystal, Stanley.** Team of Teams: New Rules of Engagement for a Complex World. Penguin, 2015.

XIV https://fas.org/irp/doddir/army/adp6_22.pdf

XV **Cohen, Philip.** Humans are hardwired to feel others' pain. New Scientist. [Online] February 19, 2004. https://www.newscientist.com/article/dn4700-humans-are- hardwired-to-feel-others-pain/

XVI **Nelson, Laura.** I feel your pain. Nature. [Online] February 20, 2004. https://www. nature. com/articles/news040216-19.

XVII **Zaki, Jamil**. The War for Kindness: Building Empathy in a Fractured World. s.l. : Robinson, 2019.

XVIII **Zaki, Jamil & Mitchell, Jason P.** Equitable decision making is associated with neural markers of intrinsic value. PNAS. 108, 2011, Vol. 49.

XIX https://www.radcliffe.harvard.edu/news/radcliffe-magazine/child-good

XX https://news.harvard.edu/gazette/story/2012/09/rapid-acts-of-kindness//https://greatergood.berkeley.edu/article/item/how_our_brains_make_us_generous

XXI **Howick, Jeremy et al.** Effects of empathic and positive communication in healthcare consultations: a systematic review and meta-analysis. Journal of the Royal Society of Medicine. 117, 2018, Vol. 7.

XXII https://my.clevelandclinic.org/podcasts/studies-in-empathy

XXIII **Howick, Jeremy** et al, 2018

XXIV University of Michigan, 2010

XXV **Zaki, Jamil.** What, Me Care? Young Are Less Empathetic. Scientific American. [Online] January 1, 2011. https://www.scientificamerican.com/article/what-me-care/.

XXVI Deloitte, 2017

XXVII **Mejia, Zameena**. Nearly 9 out of 10 millennials would consider taking a pay cut to get this. *CNBC*. [Online] June 28, 2018. https://www.cnbc.com/2018/06/27/nearly-9-out-of-10-millennials-would-consider-a-pay-cut-to-get-this.html

XXVIII https://books.google.ae/books?id=ySFlCgAAQBAJ&pg=PT18lpg=PT18&dq=John+Chambers+cisco+calls+staff+personally&source=bl&ots=EQk21lrOZr&sig =ACfU3U3E5dfpmcGQfuT_7-bvJTE4Y0vHtg&hl=en&sa=X&ved=2ahUKEwiGma7bx87pAhUxzIUKHWwFDqcQ6AEwAHoECAwQAQ#v=onepage&q=John%20Chambers%20cisco%20calls%20staff%20personally&f=false

XXIX https://www.inc.com/carmine-gallo/microsoft-ceo-satya-nadella-reveals-1-question-that-taught-him-about-empathy-and-made-him-a-better-leader.html

XXX https://en.gothiatowers.com/good-leaders-know-responsibility/

XXXI https://www.lexico.com/definition/community

XXXII Holt-Lunstad J, Smith TB, Layton JB. Social Relationships and Mortality Risk: A Meta-analytic Review. PLoS Med. 2010

XXXIII https://journals.plos.org/plosmedicine/article?id=10.1371/journal.pmed.1000316

XXXIV **Porter, Brad.** Loneliness Might Be A Bigger Health Risk Than Smoking Or Obesity. *Forbes*. [Online] January 18, 2017. https://www.forbes.com/sites/quora/2017/01/18/loneliness-might-be-a-bigger-health-risk-than-smoking-or-obesity/#21490a125d13.

XXXV **Businesssolver.** 2019 State of Workplace Empathy. [Online] 2019. https://www.businessolver.com/resources/state-of-workplace-empathy.

XXXVI **Galinsky Adam D,** et al. Power and Perspectives Not Taken. Psychological Science. 17, 2006.

XXXVII https://www.psychologicalscience.org/uncategorized/power-can-chill-the-minds-capacity-for-empathy-researchers-find.html

XXXVIII **Howe, Neil.** Millennials And The Loneliness Epidemic. Forbes. [Online] May 3, 2019. https://www.forbes.com/sites/neilhowe/2019/05/03/millennials-and-the-loneliness-epidemic/#5117b0187676.

XXXIX **Felton, J.S.** Burnout as a clinical entity—its importance in health care workers. Occupational Medicine. 1998, Vol. 48, 4.

XL **Mohney, Gillian.** Stress Costs U.S. k300 Billion Every Year. Healthline. [Online] January 8, 2018. https://www.healthline.com/health-news/stress-health-costs#1.

XLI **Porter,** 2017

XLII **Edem MJ, Akpan EU, Pepple NM**. Impact of Workplace Environment on Health Workers. Occupational Medical Health Affairs. 2, 2017, Vol. 5.

XLIII **Rovner, Laura.** What happens to people in solitary confinement. s.l. : TedxMileHigh, 2018.

XLIV **Davidson, Susan and Rossall, Phil.** Evidence Review: Loneliness in Later Life. Age UK. [Online] 2015. https://www.ageuk.org.uk/globalassets/age-uk/documents/reports-and- publications/reports-and-briefings/health--wellbeing/rb_june15_lonelines_in_later_life_ evidence_review.pdf.

XLV **Japan Times.** Japan home to 541,000 young recluses, survey finds. [Online] 2016. https://www.japantimes.co.jp/news/2016/09/07/national/japan-home-541000-young-recluses-survey-finds/#.XrGGfKhKjIV.

XLVI **Grenier, Éric.** More Canadians living alone and without children, census figures show. CBC. [Online] 2017. https://www.cbc.ca/news/politics/census-2016-marriage-children- families-1.4231163.

XLVII Eurostat. Rising proportion of single person households in the EU. [Online] 2018. https:// ec.europa.eu/eurostat/web/products-eurostat-news/-/DDN-20180706-1.

XLVIII **Holt-Lunstad, Julianne**. Loneliness and Social Isolation as Risk Factors for Mortality: A Meta-Analytic Review. Perspectives on Psychological Science. 2015, Vol. 10, 2.

XLIX https://ted2srt.org/talks/cornelia_geppert_a_video_game_that_helps_us_understand_loneliness

L **Geppert, Cornelia.** A video game that helps us understand loneliness. s.l. : Ted Salon, 2019.

LI Morning Future. Satya Nadella: when empathy is good for business. [Online] 2018. https://www.morningfuture.com/en/article/2018/06/18/microsoft-satya-nadella-empathy-business-management/337/.

LII **Hammond, Claudia.** The surprising truth about loneliness. [Online] October 1, 2018. https://www.bbc.com/future/article/20180928-the-surprising-truth-about-loneliness.

LIII **Curtin, Sally and Heron, Melanie.** Death Rates Due to Suicide and Homicide Among. CDC. [Online] October 2019. https://www.cdc.gov/nchs/data/databriefs/db352-h.pdf.

LIV https://www.businessinsider.com/cdc-teenage-gen-z-american-suicide-epidemic

LV https://www.forbes.com/sites/neilhowe/2019/05/03/millennials-and-the-loneliness- epidemic/#6581049c7676

LVI https://www.forbes.com/sites/quora/2017/01/18/loneliness-might-be-a-bigger-health-risk-than-smoking-or-obesity/#167e8cd125d1 ?

LVII University of Michigan, 2010

LVIII https://www.zerotothree.org/resources/5-how-to-help-your-child-develop-empathy

LIX Talent Works. 10 Workplace Stats You Don't Want To Miss – Infographic. [Online] August 22, 2018. https://www.talent-works.com/2018/08/22/workplace-stats- infographic/.

LX https://thedawnrehab.com/burnout-recovery-programme/

LXI https://www.hormone.org/your-health-and-hormones/glands-and-hormones-a-to-z/hormones/adrenaline

LXII **Coyle, Daisy.** How Being Happy Makes You Healthier. Healthline. [Online] August 27, 2017. https://www.healthline.com/nutrition/happiness-and-health.

LXIII Heal documentary; https://www.healdocumentary.com/

LXIV https://www.betterhealth.vic.gov.au/health/conditionsandtreatments/Hormones-cortisol-and-corticosteroids

LXV **Coyle, Daisy,** 2017

LXVI **Mohoney, Gillian**, 2018

LXVII **Malik, Nesrine**. With respect: how Jacinda Ardern showed the world what a leader should be. Guardian. [Online] March 28, 2019. https://www.theguardian.com/world/2019/ mar/28/with-respect-how-jacinda-ardern-showed-the-world-what-a-leader-should-be.

LXVIII **Zaki, Jamil.** When Cops Choose Empathy. The New Yorker. [Online] September 25, 2015. https://www.newyorker.com/tech/annals-of-technology/when-cops-choose-empathy.

LXIX Ibid.

LXX **Mesey, Christel.** Greta Thunberg's Speech to the World. [Online] December 21, 2018. https://www.gbnews.ch/greta-thunbergs-speech-to-the-world/

LXXI **United Nations.** World Youth Report. 2019.

LXXII **Kalish, Alyse.** It's True: Happy People Are Just More Productive. The Muse. [Online] June 26, 2017. https://www.themuse.com/advice/its-true-happy-people-are-just-more- productive.

LXXIII https://www.authenticyoga.nl/project/patanjali/

LXXIV **Mohney, Gillian,** 2018

LXXV **Coyle, Daisy,** 2017

LXXVI Deloitte, 2017

LXXVII **Hassard, Juliet.** The cost of work-related stress to society: a systematic. Journal of Occupational Health Psychology. 2018, Vol. 3.

LXXVIII https://hbr.org/2015/11/2015-empathy-index / https://hbr.org/2016/12/the-most-and- least-empathetic-companies-2016

LXXIX **Utton, Dominic.** How do we evoke emotion with music? The Telegraph. [Online] February 6, 2018. https://www.telegraph.co.uk/music/power-of-music/how-to-create-emotion/.

LXXX Ibid.

LXXXI **Neuroscience News.** Higher Empathy People Process Music Differently in the Brain. [Online] June 12, 2018. https://neurosciencenews.com/empathy-music-processing-9313/.

LXXXII Ibid.

LXXXIII **Ortega y Gasset, José.** *Meditations on Ortega.* s.l. : W. W. Norton and Company, Inc, 1914.

LXXXIV Ref91 – Too vague to need a reference

LXXXV **Tandon, Suneera.** Microsoft CEO Satya Nadella's leadership mantra is all about empathy. Quartz India. [Online] November 8, 2017. https://qz.com/india/1122336/microsoft-ceo-satya-nadellas-leadership-mantra-is-all-about-empathy/.

LXXXVI **Landry, Lauren.** Why Emotional Intelligence is Important in Leadership. [Online] April 3, 2019. https://online.hbs.edu/blog/post/emotional-intelligence-in-leadership.

LXXXVII **Gartland, Tom.** *Lead with Heart: Transform Your Business Through Personal Connection.* s.l. : BenBella Books, 2018.

LXXXVIII Landry, Lauren, 2019

LXXXIX Ibid.

XC Ibid.

XCI **Nishida, T.** Augmenting Conversational Enjoyment. *International Journal of Cognitive Informatics and Natural Intelligence.* 6, 2012, Vol. 4.

XCII **Krznaric, Roman.** Six Habits of Highly Empathic People. *Greater Good Magazine.* [Online] November 27, 2012.

XCIII **Bower, Tracy.** Bring on the Brilliance: The Making of Great Ideas. [Online] January 5, 2018. https://www.steelcase.com/research/articles/topics/workplace/bring-brilliance-making-great-ideas/.

XCIV **Wood, Orlando.** Lemon. How the advertising brain turned sour. s.l. : Institute of Practitioners in Advertising, 2019

XCV **Riess, Helen and Neporent, Liz.** The Empathy Effect. s.l. : Sounds True, 2018.

XCVI **Curtis, Suz.** Championing Documentary as an Empathy Machine: Tabitha Jackson Joins the Sundance Institute. IDA. [Online] January 6, 2014. https://www.documentary.org/feature/championing-documentary-empathy-machine-tabitha-jackson-joins-sundance-institute.

XCVII https://www.businesswire.com/news/home/20160712005401/en/65-Percent-Marketers-Struggle-Employ-Emotional-Marketing

XCVIII https://www.morningfuture.com/en/article/2018/06/18/microsoft-satya-nadella-empathy-business-management/337/

XCIX Ibid

C **Northwestern University,** 2016

CI https://www.who.int/health-topics/depression#tab=tab_1

CII **Krznaric, Roman**, 2012

CIII **Krznaric, Roman**, 2012

1. **Grimes, Shaunta.** Maybe we'd like each other a little bit more. [Online] 15 April 2019. https://medium.com/the-1000-day-mfa/maybe-wed-like-each-other-a-little-bit-more-1652f25f4ca4.

2. **Rifkin, Jeremy.** 'Empathic Civilization': Why Have We Become So Uncivil? Huffpost. com. [Online] 4 October 2010. https://www.huffpost.com/entry/empathic-civilization- why_b_452938.

3. **Rogers, Carl.** Empathic: An Unappreciated Way of Being. The Counseling Psychologist. 1975, Vol. 5, 2.

4. **Keen, Suzanne.** Empathy and the Novel. s.l. : Oxford University Press, 2007.

5. **Merriam-Webster.** Empathy. [Online] [Cited: 8 May 2020.] https://www.merriam-webster.com/dictionary/empathy.

6. **Roosevelt, Theodore.** Consultant's Mind. [Online] [Cited: 8 May 2020.] https://www.consultantsmind.com/2014/05/25/change-management/.

7. **Singer, Tania.** Dr. Tania Singer and the Neuroscience of Empathy.

8. **Howick, Jeremy et al.** Effects of empathic and positive communication in healthcare consultations: a systematic review and meta-analysis. Journal of the Royal Society of Medicine. 117, 2018, Vol. 7.

9. **Covey, Stephen.** *The 7 Habits of Highly Effective* People. s.l. : Simon and Schuster, 2008.

10. **Farhadi, Ashgar.** *Academy Award Ceremony.* 2017.

11. **Sisodia, Raj.** *Talking about Conscious Capitalism with Raj Sisodia.* 9 Nov 2015.

12. **Riess, Helen and Neporent, Liz**. *The Empathy Effect.* s.l. : Sounds True, 2018.

13. **Mackey, John**. Whole Foods' John Mackey on Capitalism's Moral Code. s.l. : Harvard Business Review, 17 January 2013.

14. **Denton, P K**. Small is Beautiful: The Lost Wisdom of E.F. Schumacher. [Online] 29 May 2019. https://medium.com/@peterdenton55/small-is-beautiful-the-lost-wisdom-of-e-f-schumacher-b22d6792fce.

15. **Koduru, Bhargav and Pitchuka, Balavenk**ata. The Human Side of Programming: Empathetic Leaders Build Better Teams. PharmaSUG. [Online] 2019. https://www.pharmasug.org/proceedings/2019/LD/PharmaSUG-2019-LD-150.pdf.

16. **Brooks, David.** The Empathy Issue. The New York Times. [Online] 28 May 2009. https://www.nytimes.com/2009/05/29/opinion/29brooks.html.

17. **Streep, Meryl.** Meryl Streep Promotes Empathy. s.l. : http://cultureofempathy.com/References/Experts/Meryl-Streep.htm.

18. **Ashraf, Hafsa.** Viewpoint: The world is a rainbow. [Online] 25 January 2020. https://www.dawn.com/news/1529905/viewpoint-the-world-is-a-rainbow.

19. **Porter, Brad.** Loneliness Might Be A Bigger Health Risk Than Smoking Or Obesity. Forbes. [Online] 18 January 2017. https://www.forbes.com/sites/quora/2017/01/18/loneliness-might-be-a-bigger-health-risk-than-smoking-or-obesity/#21490a125d13.

20. **Thoreau, Henry David.** *Walden.* N.C : Madison, 2012.

21. **University of Michigan.** Empathy: College students don't have as much as they used to. [Online] 27 May 2010. https://news.umich.edu/empathy-college-students-don-t-have-as-much-as-they-used-to/.

22. **Petrement, Simone.** *Simone Weil: A life.* s.l. : Pantheon, 1976.

23. **Andersen, Erika.** 21 Quotes From Henry Ford On Business, Leadership And Life. [Online] 21 May 2013. https://www.forbes.com/sites/erikaandersen/2013/05/31/21-quotes-from-henry-ford-on-business-leadership-and-life/#caecf88293c5.

24. **Kondos Field**, Valorie. Ted Talks Daily. s.l. : Bullhorn FM.

25. **Steinem, Gloria.** Gloria Steinem says Empathy is the most Revolutionary Emotion. s.l. : Culture of Empathy, 3 March 2010.

26. **Be Latina.** 3 Ways Jacinda Ardern Showed the World How to Lead a Nation Through Tragedy. [Online] 19 March 2019. https://belatina.com/3-ways-jacinda-ardern-showed- the-world-how-to-lead-a-nation-through-tragedy/.

27. **Cousineau, Tara.** Growing a Kind Mind with Imagination. [Online] 21 February 2018. https://thegreatkindnesschallenge.com/2018/02/21/thekindnesscure.

28. **McChrystal, Stanley**. *Team of Teams: New Rules of Engagement for a Complex World.* s.l. : Penguin, 2015.

29. **Davis, Jessica.** Michelle Obama's life lessons to live by. [Online] 6 March 2020. https://www.harpersbazaar.com/uk/culture/culture-news/news/a39397/25-of-michelle-obamas-greatest-quotes/.

30. **Sinek, Simon.** Leaders Put People First. [Online] 2020. https://simonsinek.com/commit/ leaders-put-people-first/.

31. **Lama, Dalai.** *The Compassionate Life.* s.l. : Simon and Schuster, 2012.

32. **Aristotle.** Happiness is the meaning and the purpose of life, the whole aim and end of human existence. *Independent.ie.* [Online] 18 January 2004. https://www.independent.ie/irish-news/happiness-is-the-meaning-and-the-purpose-of-life-the-whole-aim-and-end- of-human-existence-aristotle-26216941.html.

33. **Talbot, Amanda**. *Rethink: The Way You Live.* s.l. : Murdoch Books, 2012.

34. **Open University.** Human Interactions with the Environment. [Online] [Cited: 9 May 2020.] https://www.open.edu/openlearncreate/mod/oucontent/view. php?id=79926&printable=1.

35. **Harris, Belinda.** *Leading By Heart. School of Leadership and Management.* 2004, Vol. 24.

36. **Economy, Peter.** 7 Keys to Leading With Your Heart. *Inc.com.* [Online] 18 December 2014. https://www.inc.com/peter-economy/7-keys-to-heart-centered-leadership.html.

37. **Landry, Lauren.** Why Emotional Intelligence is Important in Leadership. [Online] 3 April 2019. https://online.hbs.edu/blog/post/emotional-intelligence-in-leadership.

38. **Tandon, Suneera.** Microsoft CEO Satya Nadella's leadership mantra is all about empathy. *Quartz India.* [Online] 8 November 2017. https://qz.com/india/1122336/microsoft-ceo-satya-nadellas-leadership-mantra-is-all-about-empathy/.

39. **Preston, Sammy.** Princess Diana's enchanting legacy: only do what your heart tells you. [Online] 25 August 2017. https://www.lifestyle.com.au/style/princess-dianas-enchanting-legacy-only-do-what-your-heart-tells-you.aspx.

40. **Giuliano, R Mark.** *Speak Easy: The secrets of successful public speaking by an expert, international speaker.* s.l. : Williams and Company, 2005.

41. Seed, John. I Asked Artists About Empathy: Here Is What They Said... [Online] 16 January 2017. https://www.huffpost.com/entry/i-asked-artists-about-empathy-here-is-what-they-said_b_587bbac0e4b094e1aa9dc740.

42. **O'Connor, Paul.** How To Win Over Customers: Lessons From 8 Rock-Star Brands. *Fast Company.* [Online] 17 January 2014. https://www.fastcompany.com/3025028/how-to- win-over-customers-lessons-from-8-rock-star-brands.

43. **Stanton, Sharon.** Why Empathy is the #1 Key to the Best Marketing. [Online] 7 May 2018. https://synecticsmedia.com/why-empathy-is-the-1-key-to-the-best-marketing.

44. **United Nations.** Goal 16: Promote just, peaceful and inclusive societies. [Online] 16 September 2018. https://www.un.org/sustainabledevelopment/peace-justice/.

CONTINUE THE CONVERSATION

Connect with Mimi on social media **@miminicklin** on Instagram, and LinkedIn and **@miminicklinleadership** on Facebook and /miminicklin on YouTube. Tune into her empathy stories podcast 'MimiYouYou' on all podcast platforms. To find out more about her keynote speaking, training and masterclasses please visit **www.miminicklin.com**.